# Microservices Architecture

Dedicated to my grandfather Binda Ray.

# Author information

For any help please contact :
Amazon Author Page :
amazon.com/author/ajaykumar
Email : ajaycucek@gmail.com ,
 ajaxreso@gmail.com
Linkedin :
https://www.linkedin.com/in/ajaycucek
Facebook :
https://www.facebook.com/ajaycucek
Youtube :
 https://www.youtube.com/channel/UC1uXEebtqCLYxVdzirKZGIA
Twitter : https://twitter.com/ajaycucek
Instagram :
https://www.instagram.com/ajaycucek/
Skype : ajaycucek

# Table of contents

1 .................................................................................................5
Author information ........................................................................5
3 .................................................................................................5
Table of contents ..........................................................................5
4 .................................................................................................5
Book Overview .............................................................................5
7 .................................................................................................5
Book Overview .............................................................................5
7 .................................................................................................5
Module 1 : Introduction ................................................................5
9 .................................................................................................5
Introduction ..................................................................................5
9 .................................................................................................5
What is a Service? .......................................................................5
11 ...............................................................................................5
Microservices Introduction ...........................................................5
16 ...............................................................................................5
The Monolithic .............................................................................5
23 ...............................................................................................5
Emergence of Microservices : Why now ? ..................................5
30 ...............................................................................................5
Emergence of Microservices : Benefits .......................................5
35 ...............................................................................................5
Microservices Design Principles: Introduction ............................5
39 ...............................................................................................5
Microservices Design Principles: High Cohesion .......................5
40 ...............................................................................................5
Microservices Design Principles: Autonomous ..........................5
44 ...............................................................................................5
Design Principles: Business Domain Centric .............................5
47 ...............................................................................................5
Microservices Design Principles: Resilience ..............................5
50 ...............................................................................................5
Microservices Design Principles: Observable ............................5

| | |
|---|---|
| 54 | 5 |
| Microservices Design Principles: Automation | 5 |
| 58 | 5 |
| Module Summary | 5 |
| 62 | 5 |
| Module 2 : Microservices Design | 5 |
| 64 | 5 |
| Introduction | 5 |
| 64 | 5 |
| High Cohesion | 5 |
| 67 | 5 |
| Autonomous : Loosely coupled | 5 |
| 73 | 5 |
| Autonomous : Ownership and Versioning | 5 |
| 87 | 5 |
| Business Domain Centric | 5 |
| 94 | 5 |
| Resilience | 5 |
| 100 | 5 |
| Observable : Centralized Monitoring | 5 |
| 105 | 5 |
| Observable: Centralized Logging | 5 |
| 109 | 5 |
| Automation: CI Tools | 5 |
| 114 | 5 |
| Automation: CD Tools | 5 |
| 118 | 5 |
| Module Summary | 5 |
| 122 | 5 |
| Module 3 : Technology for Microservices | 5 |
| 126 | 5 |
| Introduction | 5 |
| 126 | 5 |
| Communication: Synchronous | 5 |
| 127 | 5 |
| Asynchronous Communication | 5 |
| 134 | 5 |
| Hosting Platforms : Virtualization | Containers | Self Hosting | Registry and Discovery | 5 |

138 .................................................................................................. 5
Hosting Platforms: Virtualization ................................................. 5
139 .................................................................................................. 5
Hosting Platforms: Containers ..................................................... 5
144 .................................................................................................. 5
Hosting Platforms: Self Hosting .................................................. 5
148 .................................................................................................. 5
Hosting Platforms: Registration and Discovery ........................ 5
151 .................................................................................................. 5
Observable Microservices: Monitoring Tech | Logging Tech ............ 5
154 .................................................................................................. 5
Observable Microservices: Monitoring Tech ............................ 5
155 .................................................................................................. 5
Observable Microservices: Logging Tech ................................. 5
159 .................................................................................................. 5
Microservices Performance: Scaling | Caching | API Gateway ........ 5
163 .................................................................................................. 5
Microservices Performance: Scaling ........................................... 5
164 .................................................................................................. 5
Microservices Performance: Caching .......................................... 5
168 .................................................................................................. 5
Microservices Performance: API Gateway ................................ 5
171 .................................................................................................. 5
Automation Tools: Continuous Integration | Continuous Deployment
................................................................................................................ 5
175 .................................................................................................. 5
Automation Tools: Continuous Integration ............................... 5
176 .................................................................................................. 5
Automation Tools: Continuous Deployment ............................. 5
180 .................................................................................................. 5
Module Summary ............................................................................... 5
184 .................................................................................................. 5
Module 4 : Moving forward with microservices ....................... 5
186 .................................................................................................. 5
Introduction ........................................................................................ 5
187 .................................................................................................. 5
Brownfield Microservices: Approach | Migration | Database Migration | Transactions | Reporting ............................................... 5
188 .................................................................................................. 5

Brownfield Microservices: Approach .................................................. 5
189 ......................................................................................................... 5
Brownfield Microservices: Migration .................................................. 5
195 ......................................................................................................... 5
Brownfield Microservices: Database Migration .................................. 5
201 ......................................................................................................... 5
Brownfield Microservices: Transactions ............................................. 5
205 ......................................................................................................... 5
Brownfield Microservices: Reporting .................................................. 5
211 ......................................................................................................... 5
Greenfield Microservices : Introduction | Approach ......................... 5
217 ......................................................................................................... 5
Greenfield Microservices: Introduction .............................................. 5
218 ......................................................................................................... 5
Greenfield Microservices: Approach ................................................... 5
219 ......................................................................................................... 5
Microservices Provisos .......................................................................... 5
223 ......................................................................................................... 5
Microservices Architecture ................................................................... 1

Module Summary 227

# Book Overview

## Book Overview

In this book we will look at the main design principle. We will look at exactly what these design principles are and what they imply when it comes to design new software. For years people have used the style which is opposite of microservices and this unfortunately resulted into large rigid application services and overtime these large rigid applications , services and APIs become so complex that they are difficult to change and deploy without introducing risk. The phrase monolithic architecture is used to describe this large software architecture style. Microservices architecture is the solution to avoid this monolithic type style.

- Easy risk free to change
- Small scalable components
- Reduces risks during deployments
- Many other design benefits

Microservices architecture and its design principle enable us to design software that is easy risk free to change and deploy and it lets us make software architecture that is made up of small component that are each individually scalable allowing us to scale out specific component that require improved performance. This also reduces risks during deployments because we only have to deploy components that have changed instead of deploying entire software architecture each time. There are many other design benefits that microservices architecture style brings to software. In this book we will learn exactly what each one them are and exactly which design pattern to use. So at the end of this book you will learn all the design principles required to implements this architecture style and the exact approach to each one.

- Prerequisites : No prior knowledge required

# Module 1 : Introduction

## Introduction

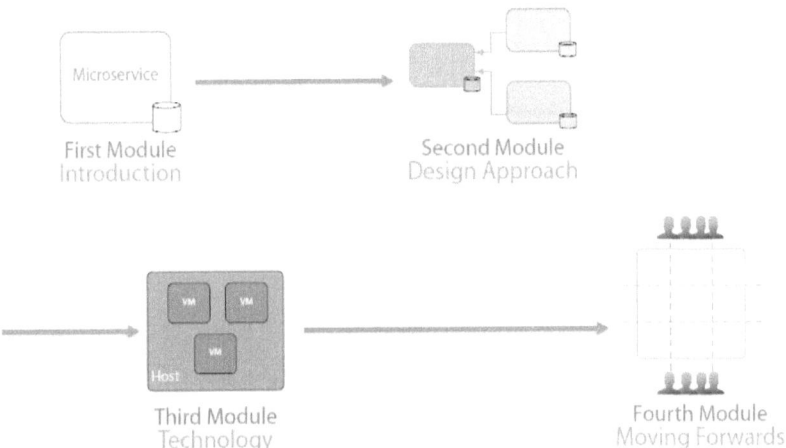

In this module we'll start off first by introducing microservices, and we will also look at what was before microservices. We will then look at the emergence of microservices, why they are so successful and useful now, and then we will conclude the module by looking at the design principles that are associated with microservices architecture.

# What is a Service?

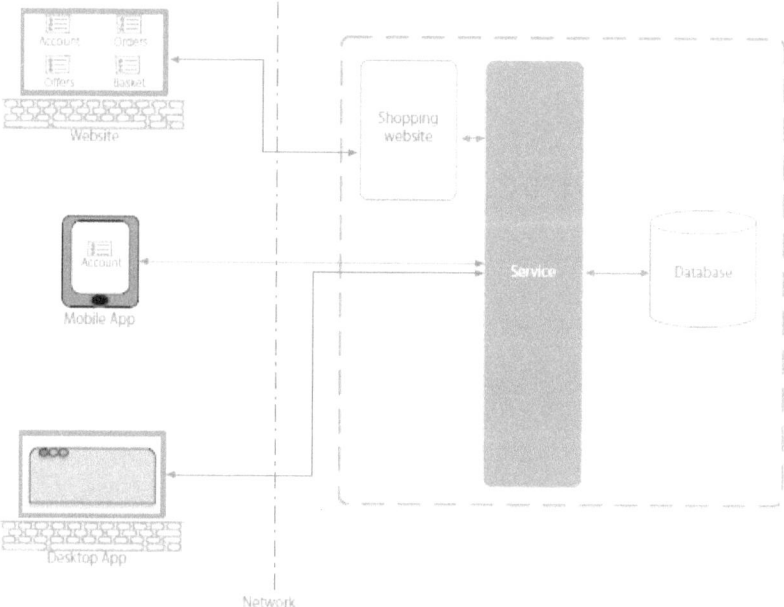

We're going to start off by introducing the microservices architecture. The first thing we'll do is we'll question what a service is, and then we'll move on to introducing the microservices architecture itself. We will finish of this section of the module by looking at monolithic architecture. This is the architecture that came before microservices. Let's start off by answering the question of what is a service. A service is a piece of software which basically provides functionality to other pieces of software within your system. It basically provides a service to other pieces of software. The other pieces of software could be anything from a website to a mobile app or a desktop app, or even another service which uses another service in order to carry out a particular type of functionality. And the service basically provides functionality to these applications, so for example, in the shopping website context, when a user places an order on the website, the website talks to the service, and the service actually carries out the creation, the update, the deletion, and the retrieval of orders from the database, so it provides functionality to the website application. And the communication between the software components and the service normally happen over a network using some kind of communication protocol. For example, a mobile app might communicate to a service via the internet. A system which uses a service or multiple services in this fashion is known to have a service-oriented architecture, and this is normally abbreviated as SOA, or SOA, and the main idea behind SOA is, instead of using \_\_\_\_\_ modules within each client application, I instead use a service to provide functionality to my client applications, and this allows me to have many client applications using the same functionality, and in the future I can have newer or different types of clients connecting to the same service, reusing that functionality, and as a software architecture, SOA has been successful.

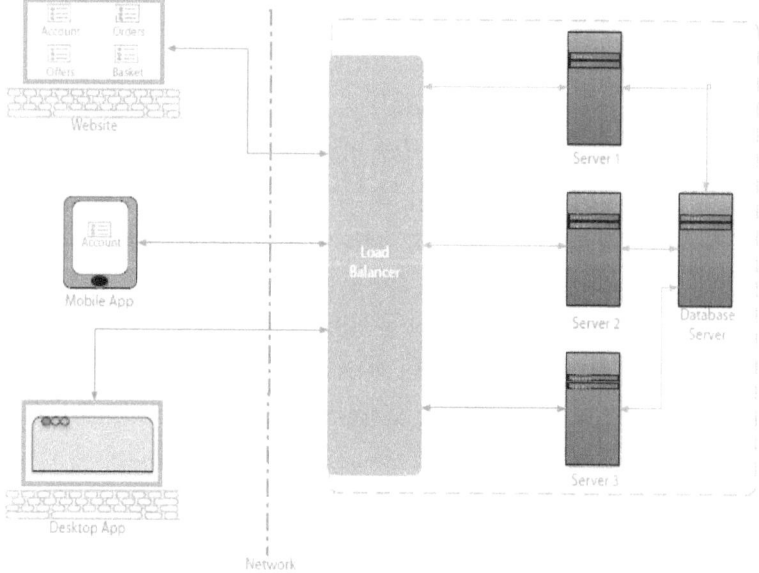

It allows us to scale up our software when demand increases by enabling us to have a copy of the service on multiple servers, so when the traffic comes in a load balancer will redirect that request to a specific instance of the service, and we can have multiple instances of the service, so when the demand increases we just increase the number of instances of the service running across servers. We have already mentioned the fact that service-oriented architecture provides reusability, reusability of functionality. So, for example, the function to create an order on a website could be the same functionality which is triggered by a mobile app on our service, so it's the same code creating an order for both the website and the mobile application, it allows us to reuse functionality. Another key characteristic of service-oriented architecture is the idea of having standardized contracts or interfaces. When our client application called the service, it called the service by calling a method. The signature of that method normally doesn't change when the service changes, so we can upgrade our service without having to upgrade our clients, as long as the contract and the interface, i.e., the signature of the method doesn't change, we do not have to upgrade our clients when we upgrade our service. Another key characteristic of a service is the fact that they are stateless, so when a request comes in from a website to our service, that instance of the service does not have to remember the previous request from that specific customer, that specific client, it basically has all the information from the request that it needs in order to retrieve all the data associated with previous requests within the service, so service does not have to remember the previous calls a client has made to that particular instance of the service, it's stateless, and therefore, any instance of the service can honor any incoming request from a client because it does not have to remember any previous interaction with any other instance of a service. Now that we know what a service is and what the service-oriented architecture is, we can start introducing the microservices architecture. The microservices architecture is basically an improved version of service-oriented architecture, and therefore it shares all the key characteristics of the service-oriented architecture, of scalability, reusability, and standardized contracts and interface for backwards compatibility, and the idea of having a service that's stateless.

## Microservices Introduction

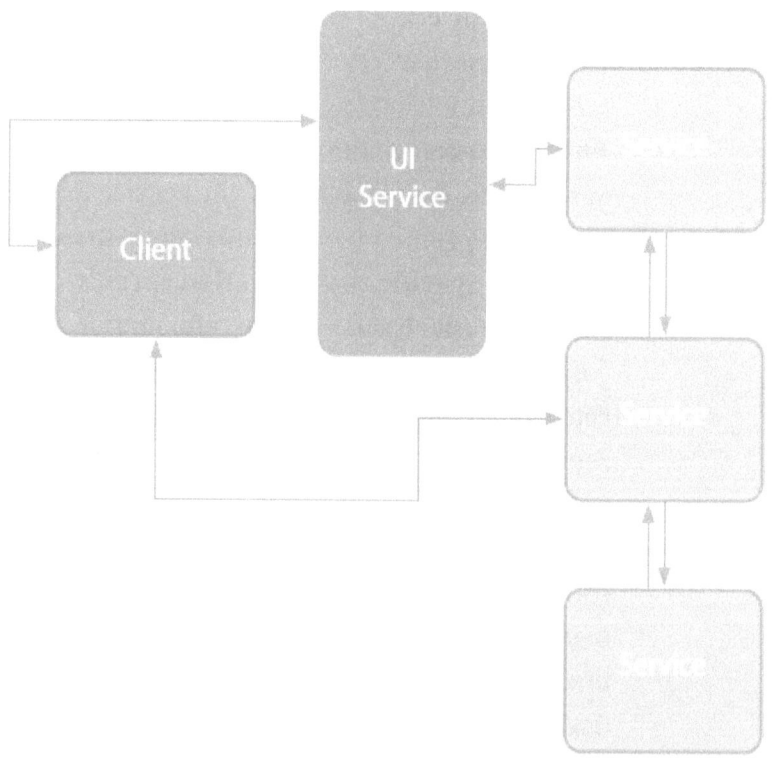

- SOA done well

- Knowing how to size a service
- Traditional SOA resulted in monolithic services
- Micro sized services provide
  - Efficiently scalable applications
  - Flexible applications
  - High performance applications
  - Application(s) powered by multiple services
  - Small service with a single focus
  - Lightweight communication mechanism
  - Both client to service and service to service
  - Technology agnostic API
  - Independent data storage
  - Independently changeable
  - Independently deployable
  - Distributed transactions

- Centralized tooling for management

In this next session of the module we're going to now introduce the microservices architecture. The microservices architecture is basically service-oriented architecture done well. After years of doing service-oriented architecture, people have realized what service-oriented architecture should be, and this is basically what microservices architecture is, it's an evolution of service-oriented architecture. Microservices basically introduce a new set of additional design principles which teach you how to size a service correctly. Because there was no guidance in the past on how to size a service and what to include in a service, traditional service-oriented architecture resulted in monolithic large services, and because of the size of the service, these services became inefficient to scale up and change in an allowable way. Smaller services, i.e., microservices, basically provide services which are more efficiently scalable, which are flexible, and which can provide high performance in the areas where performance is required. An application which is based on microservices architecture is normally an application which is powered by multiple microservices, and each one of these microservices will provide a set of functions, a set or related functions, to a specific part of the application. A microservice normally provides a set of related functions to applications, to client applications and client services. Because the microservice normally has a single focus, it does one thing and it does it well. Microservice architecture also uses lightweight communication mechanism between clients and services and service to service. The communication mechanism has to be lightweight and quick, because when you carry out a transaction within a microservices architectured system, the transaction will be a distributed transaction which is completed by multiple services, therefore the services need to communicate to each other in a quick and efficient way over the network. It needs to be a lightweight, fast communication mechanism. The application interface for a microservice, or the way you talk to a Microservice, also needs to be technology agnostic. This basically means the service needs to use an open communication protocol so that it does not dictate the technology that the client application needs to use. And by using open communication protocols, for example, like HTTP REST, we could easily have a .NET client application which talks to a Java-based microservice. In a monolithic service, you're also likely to have a central database in order to share data between applications and services. In microservices architecture, each microservice has its own data storage. Another key characteristic of a microservice is that it is independently changeable. I can upgrade, enhance or fix a specific microservice without changing any of the clients or any of the other services within the system. And because microservices are independently changeable, they also need to be independently deployable. By modifying one microservice, I should be able to then deploy that change within my system independently from everything else without deploying anything else. We've already mentioned the fact that when you make a transaction within a microservices architectured system, the transaction is most likely to be completed by multiple services, multiple services which are distributed, and therefore, your transaction is also a distributed transaction. And because a microservices architectured system has so many moving parts, there's a need for centralized tooling for management of the microservices. You need something, a tool, which will help you manage and see the health of your system because there are so many moving parts. Let's have a look at a high level architecture diagram for a microservices system.

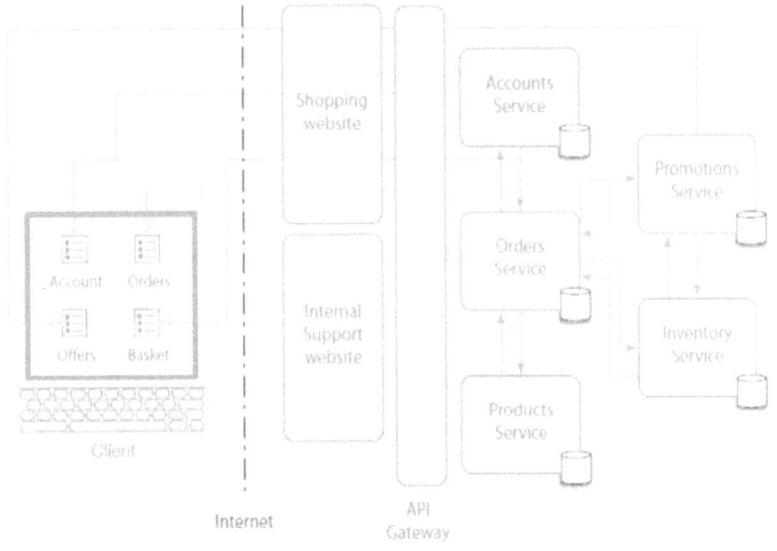

This is an example of a typical e-commerce system, and as you can see on the left-hand side our shopping website is running in the customer's browser. The browser connects to our shopping website via the internet, and our shopping website might be an ASP.NET MVC website which is running on IIS. All the processing required for all the interactions with the website is actually carried out by a number of microservices which are running in the background. Each microservice has a single focus, or a single set of related functions, and each microservice also has its own data storage and it's also independently changeable and deployable. So, for example, I could upgrade the Orders Service without upgrading any other part of my system. There might also be multiple instances for each type of microservice. For example, if the Orders Service is in demand, we might have several instances of the Orders Service in order to satisfy demand. And in order to direct a request from the shopping website to the correct instance of an order service, we have an API Gateway. We will cover the API Gateway in more detail later on, but for now think of it as something that manages and routes a request to the correct microservice within our system. So in this example, when the customer places an order the shopping website might use multiple services and multiple functions within those services, in order to satisfy that transaction. And this is why in a microservices architecture a transaction is normally a distributed transaction, because the transaction is actually satisfied by multiple pieces of software, i.e., our microservices, in order to complete the transaction, and that's why the communication between these microservices needs to be super fast and lightweight in order to complete the transaction quickly. Throughout the rest of the book you will see how design principles can be used to architect a microservices architecture like this.

# The Monolithic

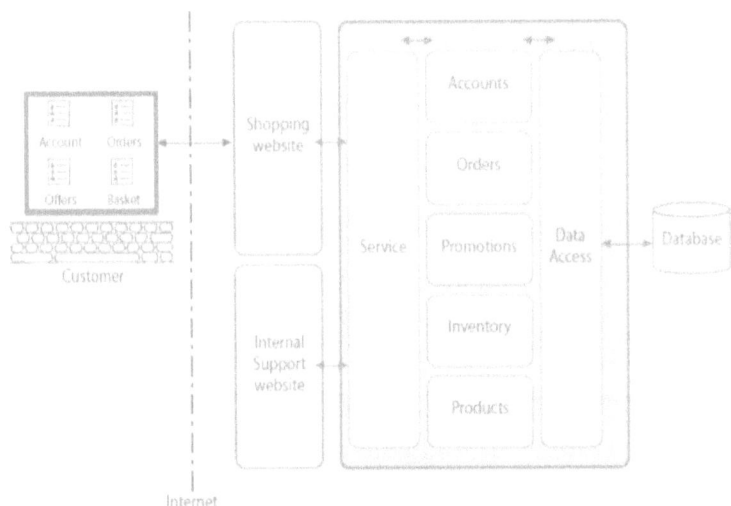

- Typical enterprise application
- No restriction on size
- Large codebase
- Longer development time
- Challenging deployment
- Inaccessible features
- Fixed technology stack
- High level of coupling
  - Between modules
  - Between services
- Failure could affect the whole system

- Scaling requires duplication of the whole system
- Single service on server
- Minor change could result in complete rebuild
- Easy to replicate environment

In this part of the module we're going to look at the monolithic type of system. This is basically the type of system that came before the microservices movement. These are large systems that almost do the opposite of what microservices are trying to achieve. So the typical monolithic system is basically your typical enterprise application, and this application might be in the form of a large website with all the modules packaged in together into one package or it could be in the form of a service which talks to a website, and the service itself is a large service with all the modules packaged together as one executable. The key characteristic is, as you add stuff to your application it keeps growing, there's no restriction in size, there's no division. There's always one package which basically contains everything, and therefore you also end up with a large code base. And because the code base is so large, it might also take the team longer to develop new functionality within the application. It might be the code is so intertwined that it's difficult to make a change without affecting other parts of the system, and therefore testing takes longer. Deployment of a large system can also be challenging, because even for a small bug fix you are having to deploy a new version of the entire system, and therefore, that creates greater risk. And because there's so much code and so much intertwined code, there might be functionality in one of our modules within our overall package that might be useful to an external system, but because it's hidden within our monolithic application it might not be exposed via the service, and you might have features in there which are not accessible. And because it's one large code base, we're also stuck with one technology stack. There might be a new technology that, for example, Promotions are part of our system _____ could do with a using, but it's a new technology which is different to our current technology stack. But because Promotions is part of the overall package, we can't use that new technology within the Promotions module, and it makes our overall system less competitive because we can't easily adopt new technologies which might give us a competitive edge. And because all the code is in one large package, we might also have high levels of coupling, which basically means if I change one part of the system, it might affect another part of the system because the code is intertwined, and this kind of coupling might be present between modules, and it might also be present between different services. So one large service might be intertwined with another large service, because if we change the signature of one service it affects the other service, and because it is one package, if a part of the system fails it could affect the whole system. For example, if the Account processes get stuck, it might affect the functionality of the overall service, it might degrade the performance of the overall service, even scaling up this service to meet demand is quite inefficient. If, let's say, for example, the Orders aspect of the system is in demand, we would have to create a copy of the whole package, of the whole service, in order to scale up just the Orders section. This basically means we need to buy more powerful servers every time we need to scale up because we are forced to scale the entire service up, instead of just the part which needs scaling up, and because the footprint of the application is so large, we might actually need to buy powerful _____ resource in order to run our entire application. We might have to place the service on a single server each time. When we do make a code change to the actual service, the time to compile the entire application will also be longer because there's just more code and there's more unit tests to run against the entire code base. The only one advantage a monolithic system has over a microservices system is the fact that you can run the entire code base on one machine, so when I'm developing and testing I could probably replicate the entire environment on my machine because it is just one thing to replicate and configure. Here we have another example of a monolithic system.

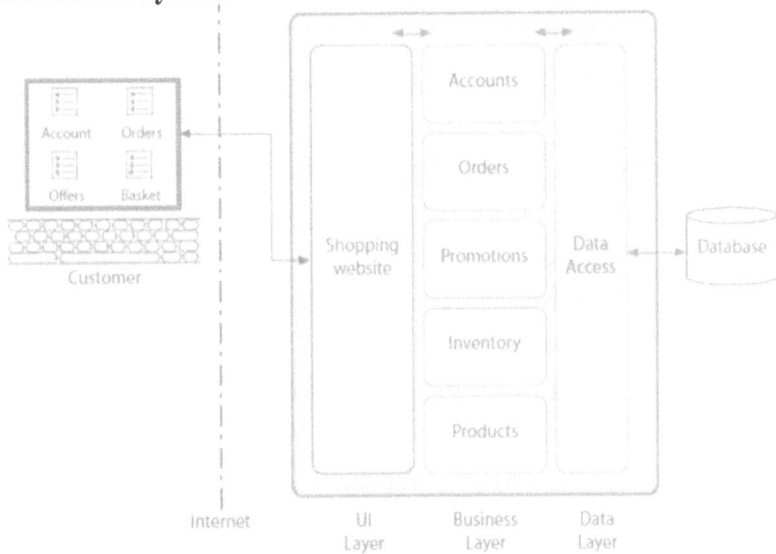

In this example we have a website application which packages in all the other modules from our system within one package. So this could be an ASP.NET MVC site where the website itself is the UI layer, and then in the Business Layer you have your accounts, all those Promotions,

Inventory, and Products namespaces which have classes related to each section. So even though you're using namespaces to divide the code within our package, the code might be still quite intertwined, basically coupled, so changing one aspect might affect another aspect, so a change in account might negatively affect Orders. For example, you might change the signature of one of the methods in the Accounts class, and because you've changed that signature, now you have to refactor the code in one of the Orders classes or in one of the Promotions classes, so this means a change that was only actually relevant to the Accounts part of the system is now impacting other parts of the system. The application might be further coupled by having one database, so for example, schema change within the database, for example, changing the data type on one column might result in several areas of the application, requiring refactoring. You can probably see now why development times are longer with a monolithic system, and why deployment is such a challenge. There is just greater risk.

# Emergence of Microservices : Why now ?

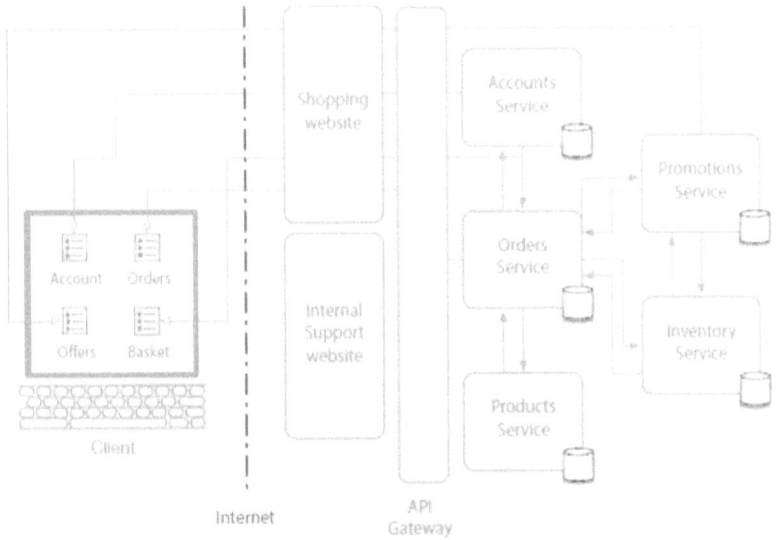

- Need to respond to change quickly
- Need for reliability
- Business domain-driven design
- Automated test tools
- Release and deployment tools
- On-demand hosting technology
- Online cloud services

- Need to embrace new technology
- Asynchronous communication technology
- Simpler server side and client side technology

In this section of the module we're going to look at the emergence of microservices, basically, why microservices architecture is useful now, and what are the benefits? One of the reasons for the microservices architecture now is the need to respond to change quickly. The software market is really competitive nowadays. If your product can't provide a feature that's in demand, it will lose market share very quickly, and this is where microservices can split a large system into parts so we can upgrade and enhance individual parts in line with the market needs. So not only do we need to change parts of our system quickly, we also need to change them in a reliable way in order to keep the market happy, and microservices provides this reliability by having your system in many parts, so if one part of the system breaks it won't break the entire system. There is also a need for business domain-driven design. The architecture of our application needs to match the organization structure, or the structure of the business functions within the organization. So if, for example, Accounts are having a massive overhaul of their software, we can just change the Account service without affecting any of the other services related to other departments. There won't be any issues between departments if one department decides to change their software, because the software architecture matches the organization structure. Another reason why microservices architecture is now possible is because we now have automated test tools. We've already seen that in a microservices architecture transactions are distributed, and therefore, a transaction will be processed by several services before it's complete. Therefore, the integration between those services needs to be tested, and testing these microservices together manually might be quite a complex task, but the good news is these automated tests automatically test the integration between our microservices, and this is why microservices architecture is now possible, because we have automated test tools which test integration between services. Release and deployment of microservices can also be complex, because remember, we now have multiple services i.e., multiple pieces of software that we need to copy to servers or onto the cloud, and it might be that for each service type we also have multiple instances that we need to upgrade at the same time. The good news is for release and deployment we also have tools, centralized tools, which can carry out this function. Another reason why so many moving parts is no longer an issue anymore is the fact that we can host them using on-demand technology. We can basically request things like virtual machines in order to host our microservices on-demand. We basically no longer need to deploy our software to physical servers. We can instead just have a server which provides a cloud on virtual machines, and we can basically just clone these virtual machines and say, deploy our microservices onto these virtual machines on-demand, requesting them in software, without having to do any physical work in order to configure and deploy the service onto a new host. On-demand hosting is even now more simple. With cloud services on the internet, you can now basically spin up a machine in the cloud without even owning a physical box, and basically host your virtual machines with your microservices running in them in a cloud service, which provides all the functionality you need to manage and monitor your microservices. Another reason for the need to adopt microservices architecture is the need to adopt new technology. Because our system is now in several moving parts, we can easily change one part, i.e., a microservice from one technology stack to another technology stack in order to get a competitive edge. Another advancement in technology which makes microservices possible is the asynchronous communication technology. In our microservices architecture when we use distributed transactions, the distributed transaction might use several services in order to complete. Using asynchronous communication, the distributed transaction does not have to wait for individual services to complete their tasks before it's complete. We will look at asynchronous communication technology in more detail in the technology module later on. Another reason why microservices architecture are possible now is the fact that we have simpler server side and client side technology. There are a number of technologies we can choose from, both at the server side and at the client side, and there are many open communication protocols which allow the server side and client side technology stacks to work together quite happily. Let's now highlight the key benefits of the microservices architecture.

# Emergence of Microservices : Benefits

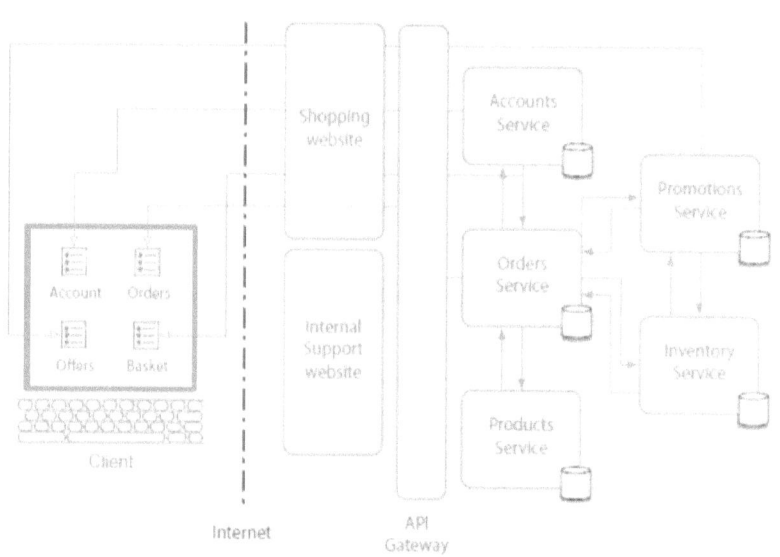

- Shorter development time
- Reliable and faster deployment
- Enables frequent updates
- Decouple the changeable parts
- Security
- Increased uptime
- Fast issue resolution

- Highly scalable and better performance
- Better ownership and knowledge
- Right technology
- Enables distributed teams

So one of the key benefits is that microservices have shorter development times. Because the system is split up into smaller moving parts, you can work on a moving part individually, you can have teams working on different parts concurrently, and because microservices are small in size and they have a single focus, the team have less to worry about in terms of scope. They know the one thing they're working on has a certain scope, and there's no need to worry about the entire system as long as they honor the contracts between the services. And because these services are loosely coupled, developers can rework, change, and deploy individual components without deploying or affecting the entire system, and therefore, deployment is more reliable and faster. Shorter development times and reliable and faster deployment also enable frequent updates. As we've already briefly mentioned, frequent updates can give you a competitive edge in the marketplace. The microservices architecture also allows us to decouple changeable parts. For example, if we know our UI for our system, our user interface for our system, changes quite often, if it uses the microservices architecture, the UI is most likely decoupled from all the services in the background, and therefore you can change it independently from all the services. Microservices architecture also increases security. In a monolithic system you might have one central database with one system accessing that database, and therefore, all you need to do is hack that one system in order to gain access to the data. In the microservices architecture, each microservice has its own database, and each microservice can also have its own security mechanism, therefore, making the data distributed and making the data even more secure. Microservices architecture also offers you increased uptime, because when it comes to upgrading the system you will probably deploy one microservice at a time without affecting the rest of the system. And because the system is split up into business domains and business functions, when a problem arises we can probably quickly identify which service is responsible for that specific business function, and therefore resolve the problem within that microservice.

Microservices architecture also makes the system highly scalable, and it gives the system better performance. When there's a specific part of the system which is in demand, we can just scale that specific part up, instead of scaling the whole system up. So if, for example, the inventory service is in demand we can create many instances of that microservice without duplicating the entire system. We can also give the ownership of a microservice to a particular development team so that there's better ownership and knowledge about the microservice. We've already briefly mentioned that microservices allow us to use the right technology for specific parts in the system, and because each microservice is separate from the other microservice, they don't share databases, and they have their own code base, you can easily have microservices being worked on concurrently by distributed teams. In the section of the module we'll start looking at the design principles that enable microservices and enable these benefits that we get from microservices.

# Microservices Design Principles: Introduction

- **High Cohesion**
- **Autonomous**
- **Business Domain Centric**
- **Resilience**
- **Observable**
- **Automation**

In this section of the module we will start looking at the design principles that make a service a microservice. I've summarized the design principles into six design principles. So in order for your service to be a microservice, the service needs to have high cohesion, it needs to be autonomous, it must be business domain centric, and it must have resilience, and it also must be observable, and automation should also be used throughout the development process. In the next few sections of the module we will cover each one of these design principles in detail and learn exactly what they mean.

# Microservices Design Principles: High Cohesion

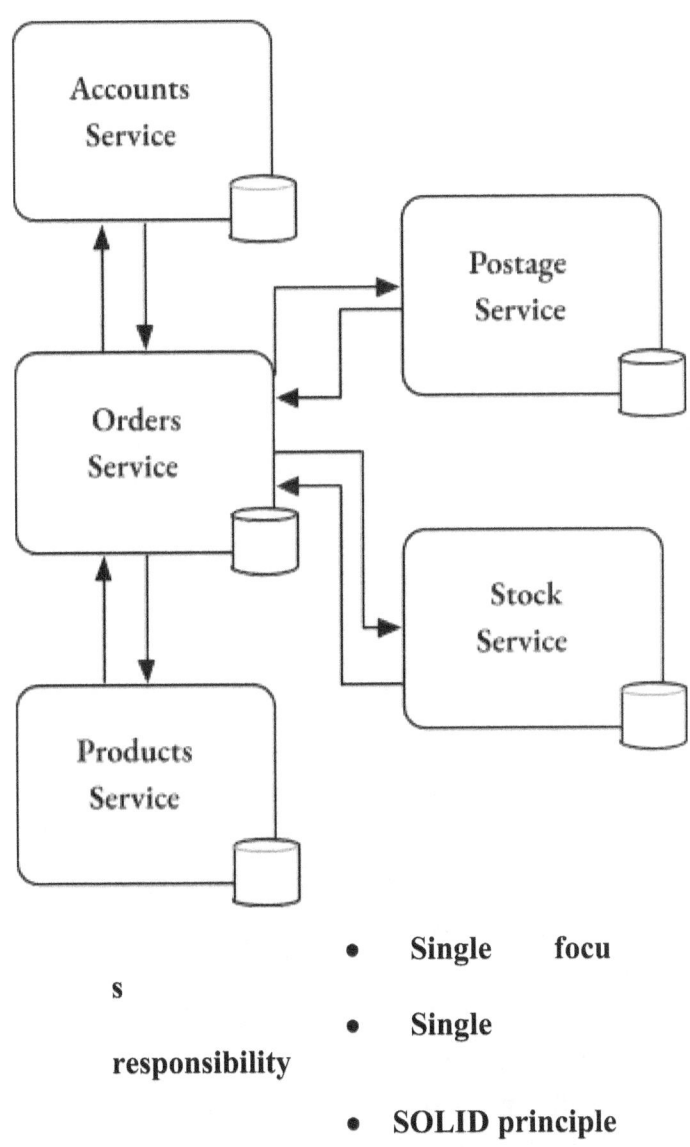

- Single focus
- Single responsibility
- SOLID principle

- Only change for one reason
- Reason represents
- A business function
- A business domain
- Encapsulation principle
- OOP principle
- Easily rewritable code
- Why
- Scalability
- Flexibility
- Reliability

So what do we mean when we say a microservice must have high cohesion? We are basically saying the microservices content and functionality in terms of input and output must be coherent. It basically must have a single focus, and the thing it does it should do well within that single focus. So, for example, you might have a microservice which has a single focus of calculating postage. So all the inputs and outputs from this microservice are solely focused on something around to do with calculating postage. And this idea of a microservice having a single focus or a single responsibility is actually taken from the SOLID coding principles, and the single responsibility principle basically states that a class can only change for one reason, and this same principle is applied to microservices. It's a useful principle because it allows us to control the size of the service, and we will not accidentally create a monolithic service by attaching other behaviors into the microservice which are not actually related. A postage service, for example, only has one reason to change. It only changes if something to do with the postage calculation or the postage logic changes with an enhance or upgrade on microservice with that new additional functionality, and the reason for change i.e., responsibility normally represents a business function or a business domain. our postage calculating microservice as a business function and an Accounts Service to do with the Accounts department might represent a business domain. High cohesion is also like the encapsulation principle from OOP programming principles. We take all data and functionality that's related and we package it into one package, which is the microservice. Because the high cohesion principle controls the size of the microservice and the scope of the contents of the microservice, the microservice is easily rewritable as we are likely to have less of an attachment to a smaller code base, and obviously there will be fewer lines of code to rewrite because the microservice will be so small. And overall, if all our microservices have high cohesion, it makes our overall system highly scalable, flexible, and reliable. The system is more scalable because we can scale up individual microservices, which represent a specific business function or business domain which is in demand, instead of scaling up the whole system, and at the same time the system is more flexible because we can change and upgrade or change the functionality of specific business functions or business domains within our system, and then we have reliability because overall we are changing specific small parts within the system without affecting other parts within the system.

# Microservices Design Principles: Autonomous

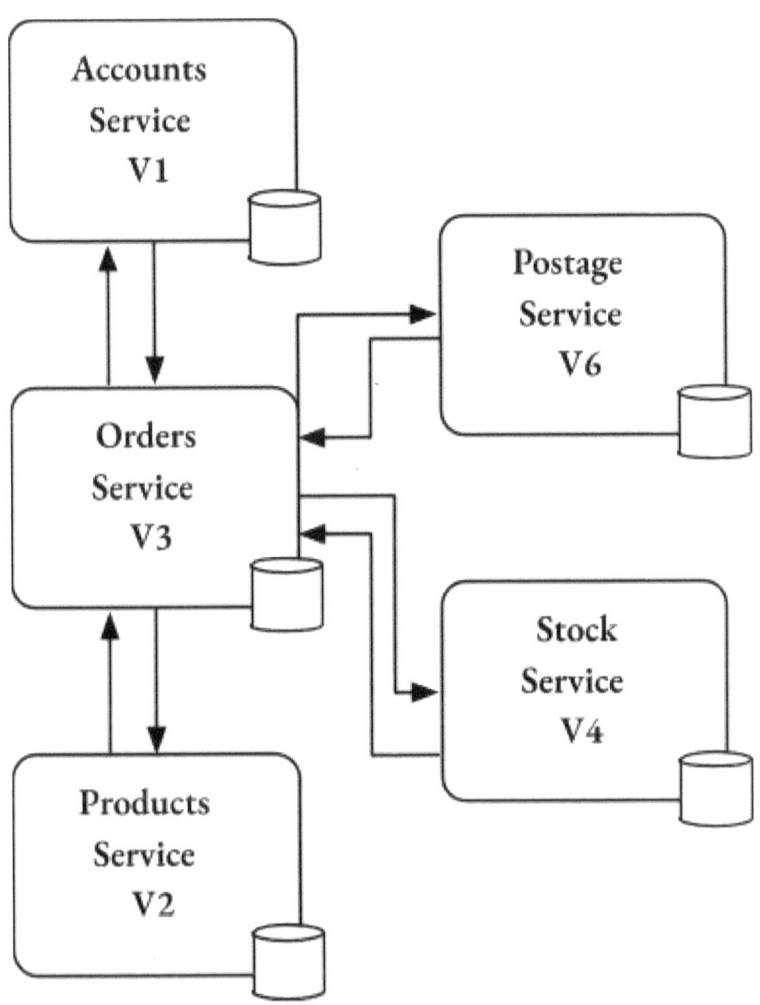

- Loose coupling
- Honor contracts and interfaces
- Stateless

- Independently changeable
- Independently deployable
- Backwards compatible
- Concurrent development

Microservices should also be autonomous. By autonomous we mean a microservice should not be subject to change because of an external system it interacts with or an external system that interacts with it. We're basically saying there should be loose coupling between the microservices and between the microservices and the clients that use the microservices, and by loose coupling we mean a change to a microservice should not force other microservices to change or other clients to change. This means microservices must honor contracts and interfaces to other services and other clients, which basically means the way the inputs and outputs are formatted for a microservice should not change between versions because that might break any other services trying to interact with that microservice using those inputs and outputs. Like a website, a microservice should also be stateless. There should be no need to remember previous interactions that clients might have had with this service or other service instances in order to carry out the current request. And because microservices honor contracts and interfaces to other services and clients, they should be independently changeable and independently deployable. They should just slot back into the system after a change or enhancement, even though it has a newer version than any of the other components within the system. This also ensures our service is always backwards compatible. Having clear defined contracts between services also means that microservices can be concurrently developed by several teams, because there's a clear definition of the input and output of a microservice. Separate teams can work on separate microservices, as long as they honor the contracts, development should go fine.

## Design Principles: Business Domain Centric

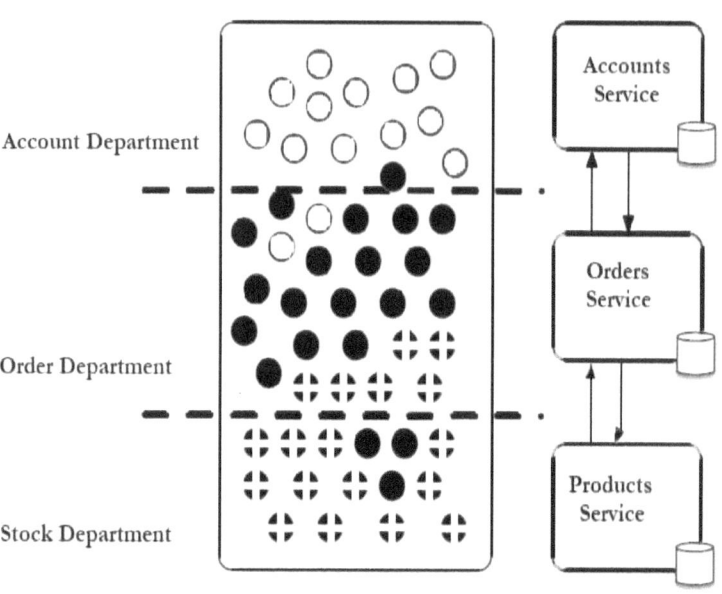

- Service represents business function
  - Accounts Department
  - Postage calculator
- Scope of service
- Bounded context from DDD
- Identify boundaries\seams
- Shuffle code if required
- Group related code into a service
- Aim for high cohesion

- Responsive to business change

A microservice should also be a business domain centric, and by this we mean a service should represent a business function. For example, in the organization you might have an Accounts department that has a lot of accounting software and accounting functionality, and this Accounts department might end up having code which results in a microservice to do an accounting functionality. You might also have specific business functions, for example, calculating postage, which might also end up within a microservice as a microservice itself. The overall idea is to have a microservice represent a business function or a business domain, i.e., a part of the organization, because this helps scope the service and control the size of the service. This is an idea which is taken from domain driven design. You basically define a bounded context, which basically contains all the functionality which is related to a specific part of the business to a business domain or a business function, and you define the bounded context by defining boundaries and seams within the code. You basically highlight the areas where related functionality exists. So, for example, on our diagram on the left you have code which is related to the Accounts department, and you have code which is related to the Orders department, and the contents within each section becomes the bounded context, and overall this will eventually become our microservice. There will be times when code relates to two different bounded contexts, and this is where we need to shuffle the code around so that the code ends up in the right place where it makes sense and it belongs in terms of business function or business domain. We need to aim for high cohesion, remember, making our microservices business domain centric, or to make our microservices responsive to business change. So as the business changes or the organization changes or functions within the business change, our microservices can change in the same way because our system is broken up into individual parts which are business domain centric. We can also change those parts which relate to specific parts in the organization which are changing.

# Microservices Design Principles: Resilience

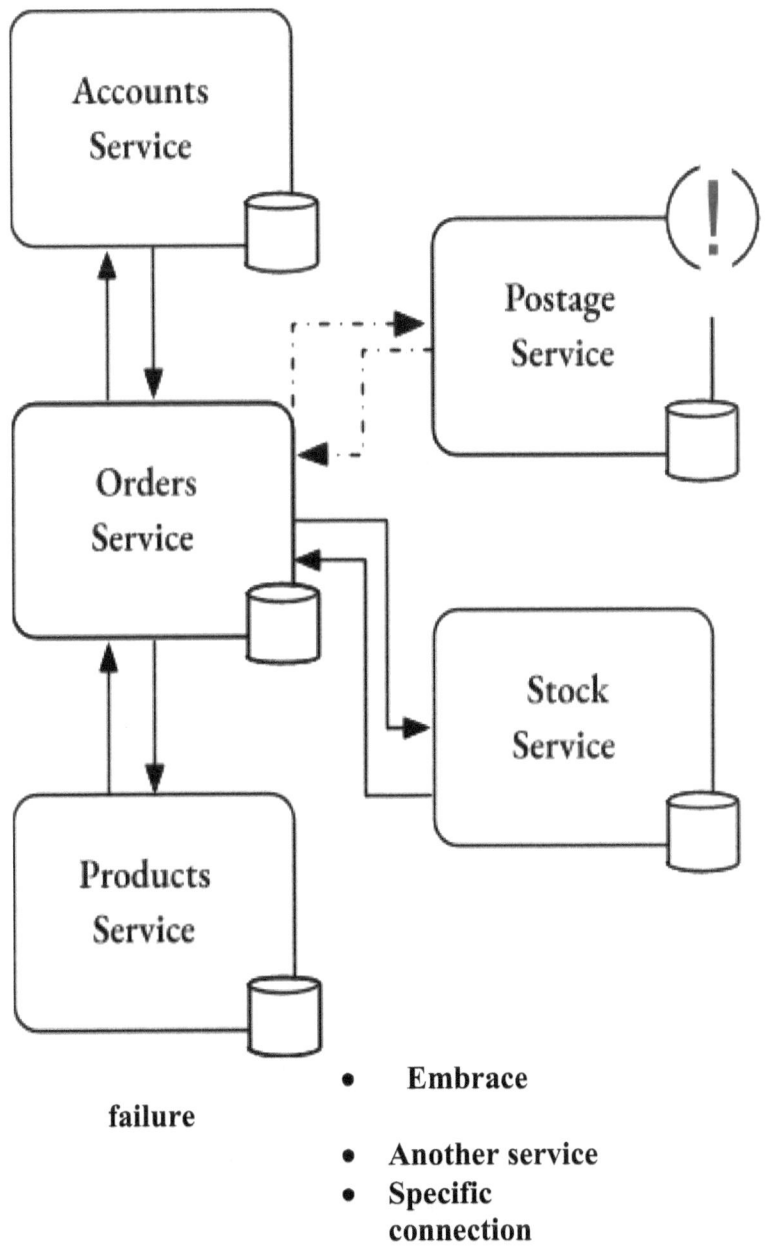

- Embrace failure
- Another service
- Specific connection

|  |  |
|---|---|
|  | • Third-party system |
| Degrade functionality |  |
|  | • Default |
| functionality |  |
|  | • Multiple |
| instances |  |
|  | • Register on startup |
|  | • Deregister on failure |
|  | • Types of |
| failure |  |
|  | • Exceptions\Errors |
|  | • Delays |
|  | • Unavailability |
|  | • Network issues |
|  | • Delay |
|  | • Unavailability |
|  | • Validate input |
|  | • Service to service |
|  | • Client to service |

Another key design principle for microservices is resilience. We basically need to embrace failure when it happens. Failure might be in the form of another service not responding to your service, or it might be a connection line to another system which has gone down, or it might be a third party system which fails to respond. Whatever the type of failure, our microservice needs to embrace that failure by degrading the functionality within our microservice or by using default functionality. An example of degrading functionality might be a scenario where we have a user interface microservice which basically draws an HTML page for available orders and promotions, but for whatever reason the promotion's microservice is down and fails to respond, so our user interface microservice basically chooses to degrade that functionality, and it chooses not to display the promotions on the page. An example of default functionality might be a postage microservice. If the postage microservice goes down and doesn't respond, and the Orders microservice relies on the Postage microservice, when it detects the fact that the Postage microservice is not responding, the Orders microservice might use a default postage rate for the order instead of retrieving one from the Postage microservice. Another way of making microservices more resilient is by having multiple instances of microservices so they register themselves as they start up, and if any of them fail they deregister themselves, so our system or our load balancers, etc., are only ever aware of fully functioning microservices. We also need to be aware that there are different types of failures. So, for example, there might be exceptions or errors within a microservice, there might be delays in replying to a request, and there might also be complete unavailability of a microservice, and this is where we need to work out if we did need to degrade functionality or if we need to default functionality. Failures are also not just limited to the software itself. You might have network failures, and remember we're using distributed transactions here where one transaction might go across the network and use several services before it actually completes, and therefore, again, we need to make our microservices resilient to network delays or unavailability. We also need to ensure that when our microservices are called and the input they receive as part of that request, that we can validate that input, and this might be input from services or from clients. We need to ensure that our microservices are resilient and can validate incoming data, and they don't basically fall over because they've received something in an incorrect format.

# Microservices Design Principles: Observable

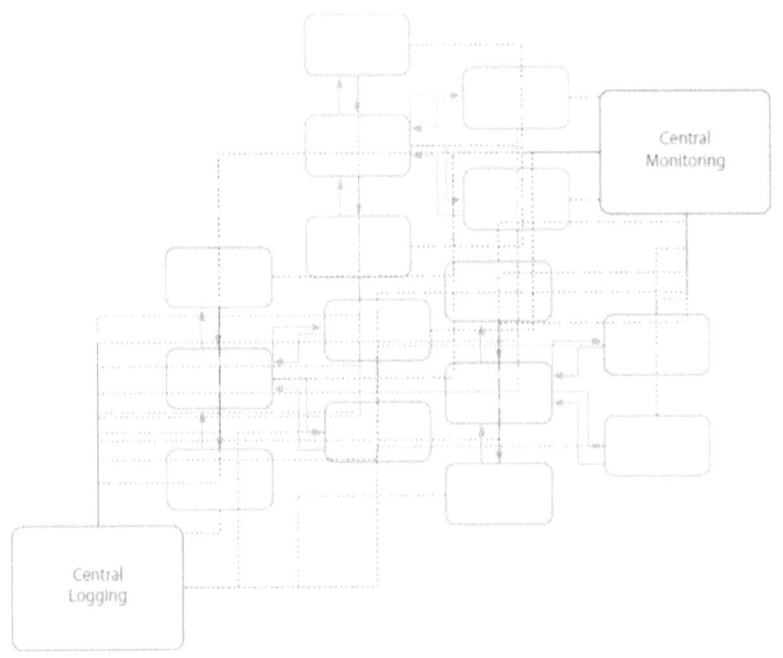

- **System health**
- **Status**

  - **Logs**
  - **Errors**

  - **Centralized monitoring**
  - **Centralized logging**
  - **Why**

- Distributed transactions
- Quick problem solving
- Quick deployment requires feedback
- Data used for capacity planning
- Data used for scaling
- What's actually used
- Monitor business data

Another key design principle that we need to build into our microservices architecture is the idea of our system being observable. We need a way to be able to observe our system's health in terms of system status, in terms of logs, i.e., activity currently happening in the system and errors that are currently happening in the system. And this type of monitoring and logging needs to be centralized so that there is one place where we need to go to in order to view this information regarding the system's health, and we need this level of monitoring and logging in a centralized place because we now have distributed transactions. In order for a transaction to complete, it must go across the network and use several services, therefore, knowing the health of the system is vital, and this kind of data will also be useful for quick problem solving because the whole system is distributed and there's a lot going on. We need a quick way of working out where a potential problem possibly lies. And because we are also using automated tools for deployment, which means our deployment will be very quick, we also need a quick way of getting feedback in response to deployment, so if there are any issues we can clearly see from a centralized place. This data collected can then also be used for capacity planning and also for scaling up our system, so when we can see that there's a clear demand somewhere within our system for a specific microservice, we can scale that area up, or when we know we've got, let's say, 100 million customers going live soon we can use this data to work out exactly how we can plan the capacity of our system in the future. We can also use this data to work out what parts of our system are actually used, and we can also build in some measures, in terms of logging, in order to measure specific things which are related to the business, for example, the number of sales on a daily basis. We can all log this to our central logging system and view this from a centralized place.

# Microservices Design Principles: Automation

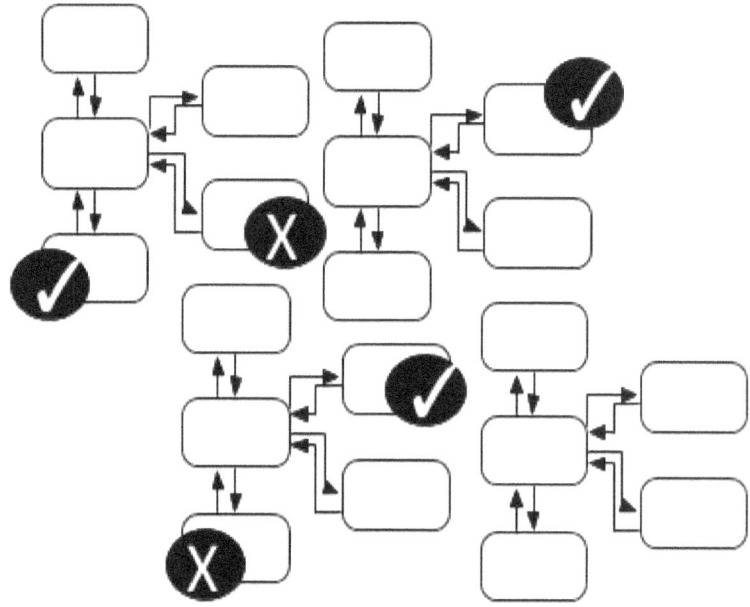

- Tools to reduce testing
    - Manual regression testing
    - Time taken on testing integration
    - Environment setup for testing
- Tools to provide quick feedback
    - Integration feedback on check in
    - Continuous Integration
- Tools to provide quick deployment
    - Pipeline to deployment
    - Deployment ready status
    - Automated deployment
    - Reliable and Continuous deployment

- -Why
  - Distributed system
  - Multiple instances of services
  - Manual integration testing too time consuming
  - Manual deployment time consuming and unreliable

We also need to feature automation in our microservices architecture, automation in the form of tools, for example, tools to reduce testing. Automated testing will reduce the amount of time required for manual regression testing, and the time taken to test integration between services and clients, and also the time taken to set up test environments. Remember, in a microservices architecture our system is made up of several moving parts, and therefore testing can be quite complex, and this is where we need testing tools to automate some of that testing. We need tools, automated testing tools which give us quick feedback, so as soon as I change the microservice and check that we have called into our _____ control system, I want these test automation tools to provide me feedback on integration, to give me confidence that my change integrates with the entire system, and this type of testing, this type of automated testing, which tests for integration, is known as continuous integration. As well as automation tools to help with testing, we need automation tools to help with deployment, a tool which basically provides a pipeline to deployment. It gives our microservice a deployment ready status, so when you check a change in, the tests pass, and then the deployment status is at ready, and then the tool knows that this build of the microservice is now ready for deployment. So not only does this tool provide a pipeline with a status for each deployable build of a microservice, it also provides a way of actually physically moving the build to the target machine or the target cloud system, so the physical deployment of the software will be all automatic, and therefore it will be reliable because it's preconfigured with a target where the software needs to go, and it will be configured and tested once, and therefore it should work every time. The idea of using automation tools for deployment falls under a category called continuous deployment. So in order to have automation, we need to use continuous integration tools and continuous deployment tools, because in a microservices architecture we have a system which is a distributed system, and there are multiple instances of the services. This is a much more complex system, and the way it's organized across our system, \_\_\_\_\_ \_\_\_\_\_ with such a distributed system manual integration testing would be too time consuming, and manual deployment will be too time consuming and unreliable.

## Module Summary

- Microservices
- Service
- The Monolithic

- Emergence of Microservices
- Why Now?

- Benefits
- Microservices Design Principles
  - High Cohesion
  - Autonomous
  - Business Domain Centric
  - Resilience
  - Observable
  - Automation

In this module we introduced what microservices are. We first started off by looking at services themselves, and we looked at how microservices have evolved from services. We then went on to see what came before microservices. This is the monolithic type of system, a system with a large code base, a system that's normally one whole large package. We also looked at why the microservices architecture is relevant now, and the main benefits of the microservices architecture in today's world. We then concluded the module by looking at the design principles that make a system a microservices architecture. We concluded that a microservice needs to have high cohesion, it needs to be autonomous, and it must be business domain centric, and it must have some kind of resilience, and the microservice alright must be observable, and there needs to be some degree of automation within the microservices architecture. In the next module, we will look at the design approach you need to take in order to apply these design principles to your architecture in order to make it a microservices architecture.

# Module 2 : Microservices Design

## Introduction

- Microservices Design
    - Principles
    - Approach

In this module, we will look at the design approach for each one of the microservices design principles. We will start off by reminding ourselves what the design principles are, and for each one we will look at the design approach we can take to implement the principle.

- High Cohesion

- Single thing done well
  - Single focus

- Autonomous

  - Independently changeable
  - Independently deployable

- Business Domain Centric

  - Represent business function or represent a business domain

- Resilience

  - Embrace Failure
  - Default or degrade functionality

- Observable

  - See system health
  - Centralized logging and monitoring

- Automation

  - Tools for testing and feedback
  - Tools for deployment

Let's remind ourselves what the design principles are. Our microservice must have high cohesion, it must do a single thing and it should do it well. It should have a single focus. This helps control the size of the microservice. A microservice should also be autonomous. It should be independently changeable and deployable, because this lets us upgrade specific parts of our system without brining risk to any other parts. Microservices also should be business domain centric. A microservice should represent a business function or represent a business domain. This is because microservices should be in line with the overall organization structure. This will mean, if specific departments change and their systems change, the change does not affect other departments and their systems, i.e., their microservices. Microservices should also have resilience. They should embrace failure and default or degrade functionality when failure occurs. This is so our overall system doesn't fail because one of the microservices has stopped working because it's waiting for a response from a third party system or another service which has gone down. Our microservices systems should also be observable. We should be able to see the overall system health, and there should be centralized logging and monitoring. This is because the microservices architecture can be complex because there are so many moving parts, therefore, we need a way of quickly problem solving when things go wrong. Microservices architecture should also have automation. We should have tools for testing and feedback and tools for deployment. This, again, is because microservices architecture can be complex. There can be many microservices and many instances of microservices, and we need tools to test the integration between these microservices and to help with the deployment of these microservices into the production environment. In the remaining parts of the module, we will look at each one of these principles in detail and the design approach we need to take in order to implement each one of these design principles.

## High Cohesion

- Identify a single focus
    - Business function
    - Business domain
- Split into finer grained services

Avoid "Is kind of the same"

- 
- Don't get lazy!

Don't be afraid to create many services

- 
- Question in code\peer reviews

- Can this change for more than one reason

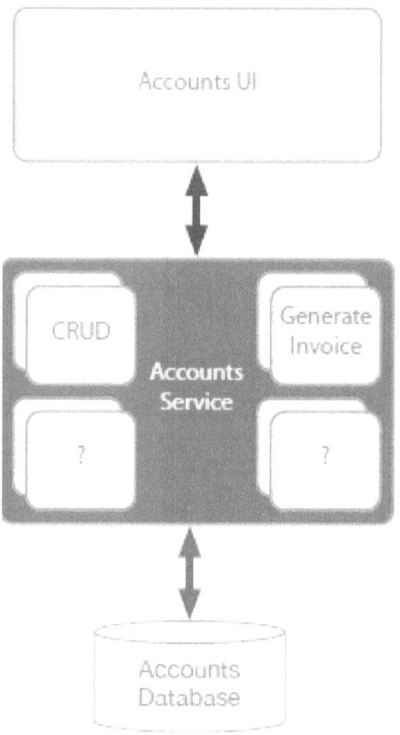

Let's start off with the high cohesion design principle. How do we implement a microservice with high cohesion? The first thing we need to do is we need to identify a single focus for our microservice. This might be in the form of a business function, for example, for Account system, generate an invoice, a function which has clear inputs and outputs. Or it might in the form of a business domain where the microservice's focus is in the form of creating, retrieving, and updating, deleting data related to a specific part of the organization, for example, the Accounts Department. The key thing is, we do not crowd our microservice with both types of focus in one microservice. For example, the diagram above, Accounts Service does all the CRUD operations to do with the data for the Accounts Department, and it also generates invoices for the Accounts Department. The Generate Invoice business function here, although it's associated with the Accounts Department it should really have its own microservices because it has its own clear inputs and outputs. It should be its own microservice with its own database to store the invoicing data.

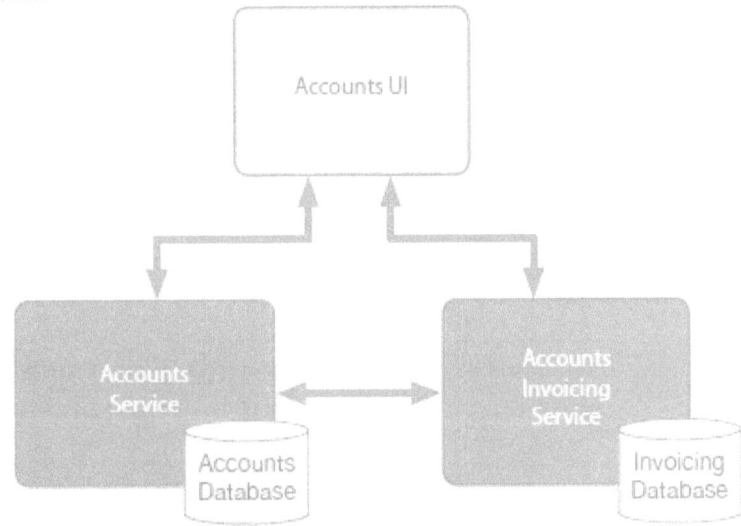

And we can now create and retrieve our general accounts data using our Accounts Service, which has a separate database, and therefore, if we make changes to the Accounts database schema, like for example, adding a new column, this does not affect our Accounts Invoicing functionality. We must also be ready to split our microservices further if, for example, our inputs and outputs on the microservice change.

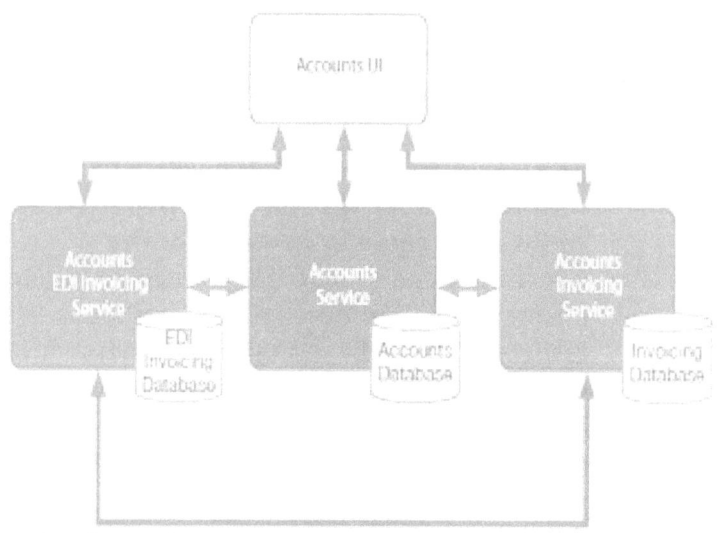

Our business function of generating an invoice might have an additional requirement of generating an invoice and sending it via EDI, via electronic data interchange, and therefore, instead of building that functionality into the existing microservice, we should really create a separate microservice which carries out that extra functionality. The two microservices can then work together in order to achieve the goal of sending an invoice via electronic data interchange. The EDI Invoicing Service can also store the EDI formatted data in a separate database, and then in the future if the EDI interface ever changes we only have to change one of our microservices, and then there's no risk of breaking the old Accounts Invoicing Service. What we need to do is when we're looking at the single focus of a microservice is to avoid the thinking of, it's kind of the same business function, and then coupling multiple business functions into one microservice. A microservice should only have one reason for it to change. This is because we want to avoid the change in one business function breaking another business function. And in our EDI example we don't want the EDI format change to change our General Invoicing functionality. We also need to avoid getting lazy, because creating an extra microservice or splitting an existing microservice will require extra effort, but you've got to remember the overall objective. Our overall objective is to have a system which is scalable, flexible, and reliable. We want our system to be in separate parts so we can enhance and deploy specific parts, and the laziness to create multiple microservices will only result in a system which is basically a monolithic system, and it will have all the disadvantages which we discussed earlier that have to do with monolithic systems, so don't be afraid to create many services. And remember you won't create thousands of microservices overnight. This will probably happen in an incremental way, and therefore you will have time to learn how to maintain and monitor these microservices. And overall, to ensure your microservices have high cohesion, continuously question the design of microservices, and this can be done in code reviews or peer reviews where you question if a new microservice has one reason to change.

## Autonomous : Loosely coupled

- Loosely coupled

- Communication by network
  - Synchronous
  - Asynchronous
    - Publish events
    - Subscribe to events
- Technology agnostic API
- Avoid client libraries
- Contracts between services
  - Fixed and agreed interfaces
  - Shared models
  - Clear input and output
- Avoid chatty exchanges between services
- Avoid sharing between services
  - Databases
  - Shared libraries

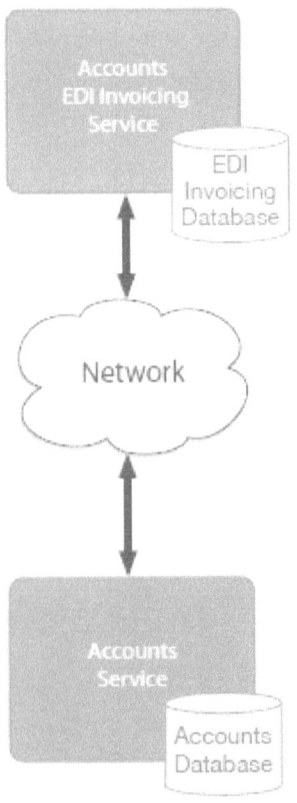

For our microservices to be autonomous, i.e., independently deployable and changeable, our microservices should be loosely coupled. Basically, our microservices should depend on each other in a minimal way, and they should have the least amount of knowledge of each other, and this can be achieved by having our microservices communicate to each other over the network, a bit like how machines are connected to each other over a network. They are not physically connected to each other directly, but the use a network in order to talk to each other, and this communication can be synchronous where the microservice calls another microservice and then waits for a reply.

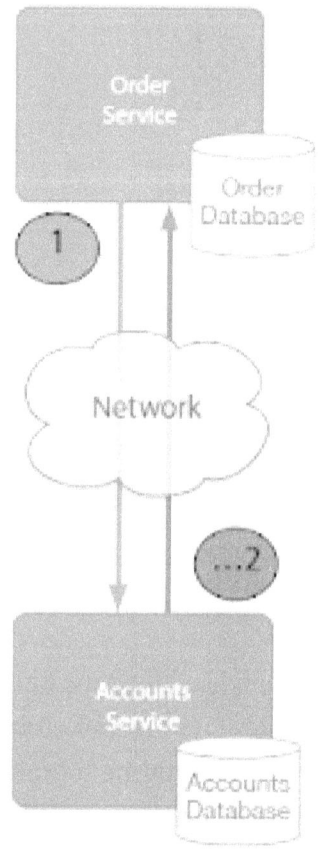

The good thing with synchronous communication is, that we know our communication is successful because we receive a response in response to our request. To make synchronous communication decoupled, the service that's being called should respond straight away, even before it's completed the actual task for the request. This is so the microservice that's making the request can carry on with other stuff whilst the task is being processed. Once the task is complete, the service which has completed the task calls back the original microservice that made the request in order to notify that the task is complete, and in order for this to work, the original request from the microservice should include a callback address. This is so that the microservice that has completed the task knows exactly which microservice to call back in order to notify it that the task is completed. To make our microservices architecture even more decoupled, we could instead use asynchronous communication.

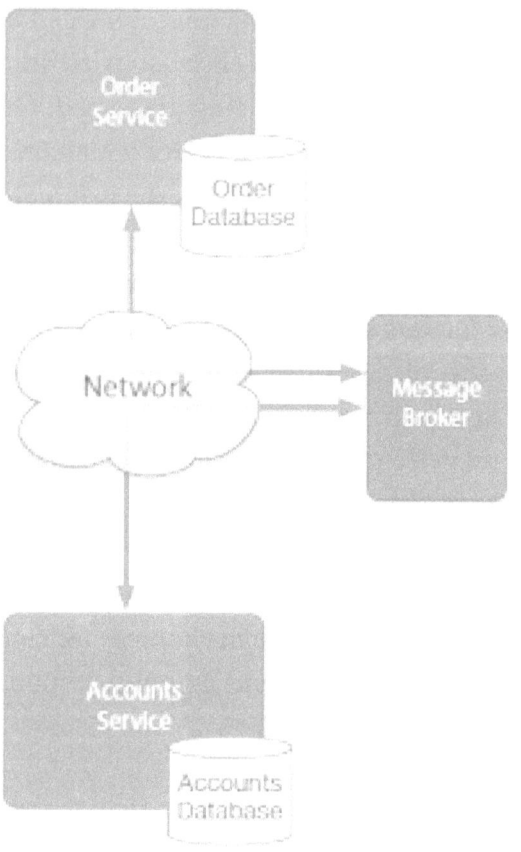

This is where instead of making requests, you instead publish events, and these events are then handled by a message broker, and then other services listen out for these events and carry out the tasks. This is the most decoupled way of communication. Instead of microservices talking to each other directly, they instead publish events in the form of messages on a message queue. Then interested microservices then pick up these messages, i.e., events from the message queue and process them. Then when the task is complete the microservice which has completed the task will publish another event in the form of a message on the message queue, which the original microservice will pick up in order to learn the fact that the task has been completed.

In order to ensure our microservices are further decoupled in terms of technology, we should use Open Communication Protocols so that we have a technology agnostic API, basically, one technology stack doesn't force other microservices to have the same technology stack. For example, by using Open Communication Protocols like REST over HTTP, we could have a .NET-based service talk to a Java-based service.

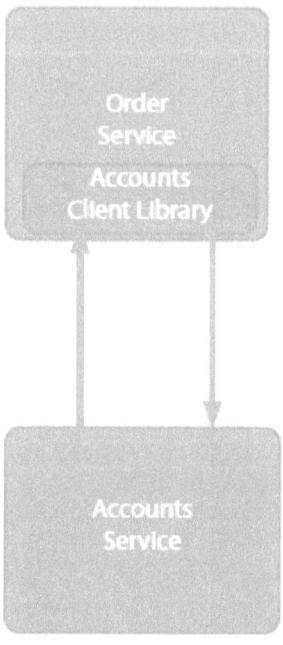

To further decouple our microservices, we should also avoid the use of client libraries. This is where the consumer of your microservice requires the implementation of a client library which you've provided in order for that consumer to talk to your microservice. Client libraries increase coupling, because if your microservice changes and it changes its client library, the consuming microservice will also need to change the implementation of the client library. The use of client libraries can also force the use of a specific technology platform at the consuming end.

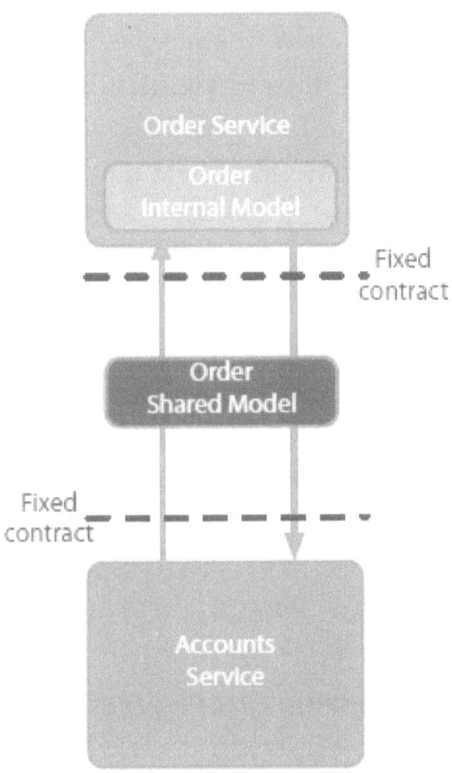

Microservices that talk to each other also should have contracts between the services. This is basically fixed and agreed interfaces between the two services. This is so when microservices change, i.e., they are enhanced or modified, the consumers don't have to change, because the way of talking to the service still remains the same. This is in terms of method signatures and the format of the data that's exchanged, and when exchanging data, always use shared models. Shared models of the data are unlikely to change when the microservices are enhanced. The shared models should be different from the internal representation of the data within the microservice. So, for example, if we add an extra field to our Order Internal Model, a field that's not actually required by the Account Service, we do not add this extra field to our Order Shared Model, and the Account Service will carry on working because our contract remains intact, and it doesn't have any surprises in terms of a new piece of data that it doesn't understand. So always keep the internal representation of data separate from data that's exchanged by using shared models to transfer the data. Agreed contracts and interfaces are also important so that when multiple teams are working on different microservices they clearly know the inputs and outputs for each microservice.

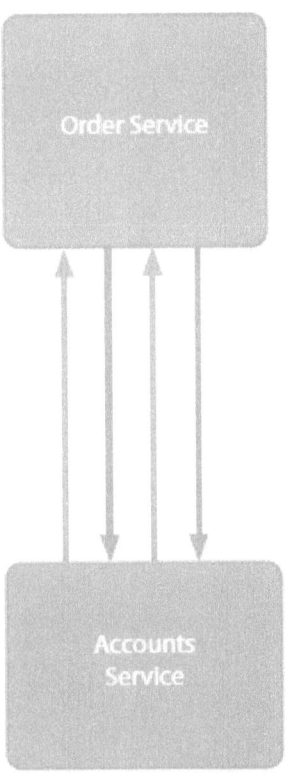

To further keep our microservices decoupled, we should also avoid chatty exchanges between two microservices. Too many exchanges between two microservices in order to complete a task, further couples the two microservices, because a change at one end might change the sequence of the exchanges at one end, and therefore forcing the other end to also change in order to cope with the change in exchanges

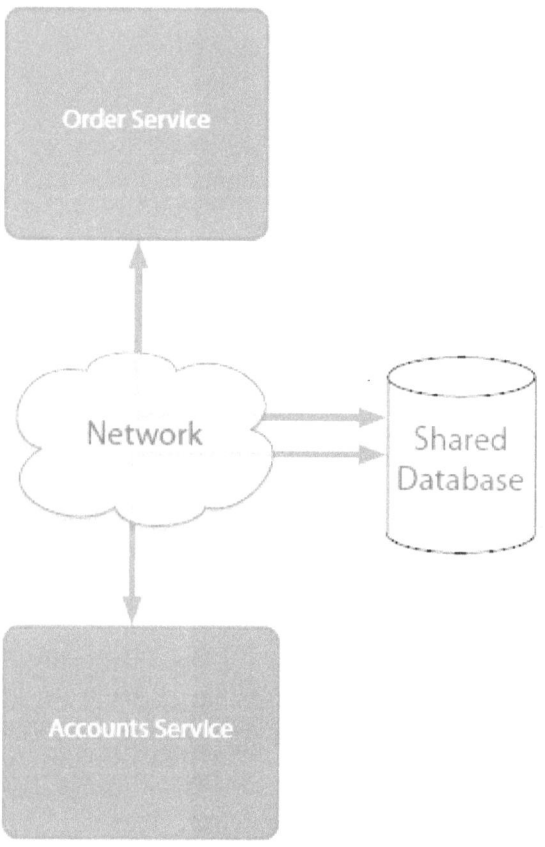

The sharing between two microservices should also be avoided, especially when it comes to sharing things like databases. Sharing a database might seem like a good idea in order to share data quickly between two microservices, but a change in a shared database will result in probably both microservices having to be changed in order to cater for the new schema change, and therefore, you'll have to deploy two microservices instead of one because of one change. It also forces our microservices to use the same database technology. If each microservice has its own database, we can use specific database technology that's suitable for that specific microservice. Data, instead, should be shared by microservices calling each other and sending the data. We should also minimize the use of shared libraries within microservices because a bug fix in a shared library might mean we have to redeploy two microservices because they carry the same bug. If there is a demand for a functionality in the form of a shared library, maybe that function itself should be a microservice which could serve other services. In the next section of the module, we will look at how versioning can be used to make our microservices more autonomous.

## Autonomous : Ownership and Versioning

- Microservice ownership by team
    - Responsibility to make autonomous
    - Agreeing contracts between terms
    - Responsible for long term maintenance
    - Collaborative development

- Communicate contract requirements
- Communicate data requirements

- Concurrent development

- Versioning

  - Avoid breaking changes
  - Backwards compatibility
  - Integration tests
  - Have a versioning strategy

    - Concurrent versions

      - Old and new

    - Semantic versioning

      - Major.Minor.Patch (e.g. 15.1.2)

    - Coexisting endpoints

      - /V2/customer/

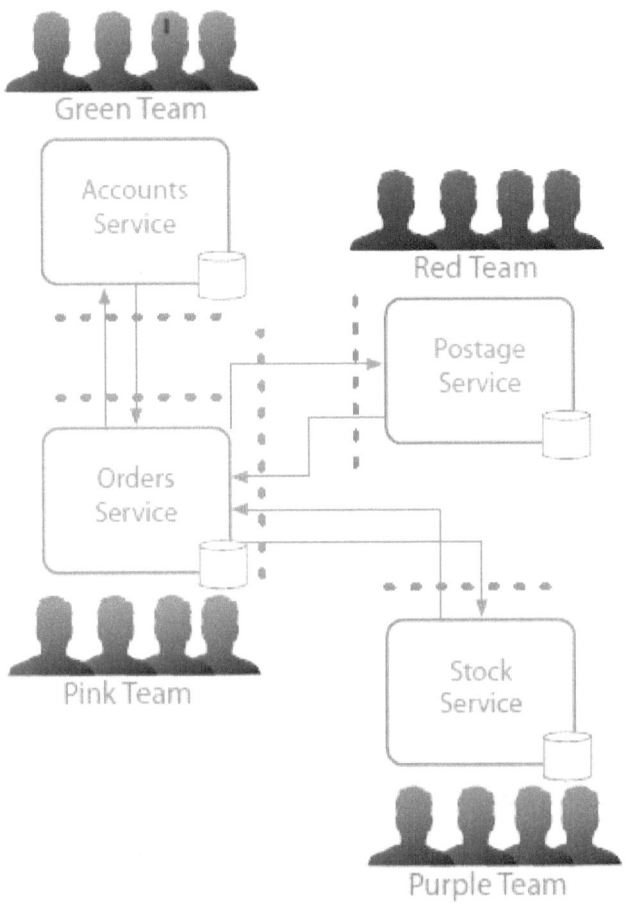

Another way of making microservices autonomous is by having them owned by a team. If small teams are responsible for microservice, i.e., they own the microservice, there will be better knowledge retention about the microservice, and also you can make the team responsible to make the microservice autonomous. It's the team's responsibility to design the microservice so that it's independently changeable and independently deployable. The teams can also be responsible for agreeing the contract between the microservices, other microservices that interact with their microservices. If a team owns a specific microservice, they will also maintain the contract so that future changes don't break contracts with other microservices. Teams that own specific microservices should also be made responsible for the long-term maintenance of that service. Ownership of the microservice will also encourage the team to collaborate more with other teams in order to communicate contract requirements and communicate data requirements. Team ownership will also encourage concurrent development. Multiple teams can work on different microservices at the same time, and agree all the interactions between them, between the teams. We have already mentioned the fact that autonomous microservices must be independently changeable and independently deployable. This means when we create a new version of a microservice, we need to think about our versioning strategy for that microservice.

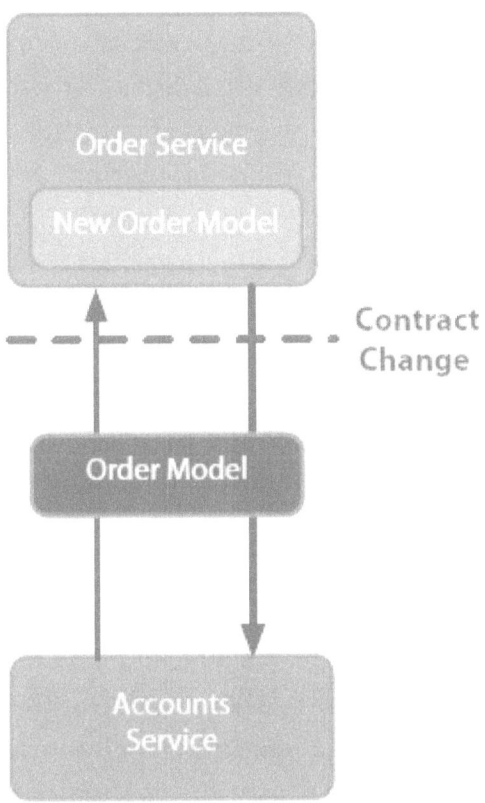

The key thing is when we create a new version of a microservice that we avoid breaking changes. Other services that consume our microservice must not break because we've changed something in the new version of the microservice. Our primary goal should be that all new changes and enhancements are backwards compatible. Microservices that used to use our microservice that's been upgraded, should carry on working without any change. We should honor the original contract that was agreed, and in order to ensure that you're new microservice doesn't break any existing contracts, you should use integration tests, integration tests which basically test the changed microservice for inputs and outputs, and shared models, basically, testing to see if the original contract is still intact. Sometimes, however, you can't avoid breaking changes, maybe because you've rewritten a microservice, and its inputs and outputs have substantially changed, and this is where you need to have a versioning strategy. So if your new version of the microservice includes breaking changes, you could have concurrent versions of the microservice running. You could have an old version and a new version running at the same time. This is especially required when you have no control over the consuming microservices and you have to have the old version of your microservice in place in order to ensure that the consuming microservices carry on working. Over time you can then slowly negotiate the migration of the consuming microservices from the usage of the old microservice to the usage of the new microservice. To make transparent what versions of the microservice are backwards compatible, we should use semantic versioning where the version number is made up of three numbers, Major.Minor.Patch. You increment the major number if the new version of the microservice is not backwards compatible, and you only increment the minor number if the new version of the microservice is actually backwards compatible, and you increase the patch number if the only change in the new version of the microservice is the defect fix and the overall microservice is still backwards compatible. Sometimes we may choose to include both the old code and the new code in the new version of the microservice. This is where we can have coexisting endpoints. So you have the original endpoint which points at the original code, the old version of the code, and you have a new endpoint which points at the new version of the code. Your consumers can then slowly migrate over time from using the old endpoint to using the new endpoint. You could even have a new version of a microservice which has the old endpoint, but the old endpoint is basically a wrapper for the new endpoint, so although existing consumers can call the old endpoint, the old endpoint basically redirects the calls to the new endpoint. It's basically a wrapper for the new endpoint. So, overall, when we say microservices need to be independently changeable and deployable, we need to ensure that when we do create a new version of a microservice it does not break existing contracts and existing microservices that consume our new microservice.

# Business Domain Centric

- Business function or business domain
- Approach
    - Identify business domains in a coarse manner
    - Review sub groups of business functions or areas
    - Review benefits of splitting further
    - Agree a common language
- Microservices for data (CRUD) or functions
- Fix incorrect boundaries
    - Merge or split
- Explicit interfaces for outside world
- Splitting using technical boundaries
    - Service to access archive data
    - For performance tuning

|                    |                    |
|--------------------|--------------------|
| Accounts Domain    | Marketing Domain   |
| Sales Domain       | Sales Domain       |

**The Business Domain Centric design principle for microservices basically suggests a microservice should represent a business function or a business domain, and the approach should be initially we define these business domains in a coarse manner and these business domains will most likely represent a department or an area within the organization. We then need to further split these areas into possible business functions or business areas.**

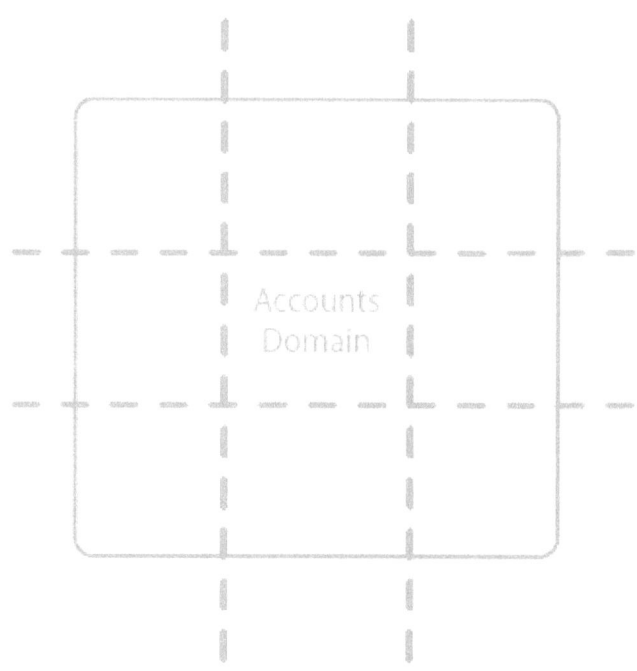

It might be that the business domain is so simple that one microservice can contain all the functionality required for that business domain, and further splitting is not required, and therefore we need to review the benefits of splitting the microservice further. A key thing to remember at the same time is the other design principle of a microservice having high cohesion. A microservice must do one thing and do it well. It must have a single focus, and only one reason for it to change. _____ from microservices as components, maps to different components, and functions within the organization, so when certain parts of the organization change we know which specific microservices to change. Also, when mapping our microservices to our organization, it's also key to agree a common language. So if, for example, we have a business function to deal with EDI Invoicing, we must ensure we call our microservice to do the functionality, the EDI Invoicing microservice.

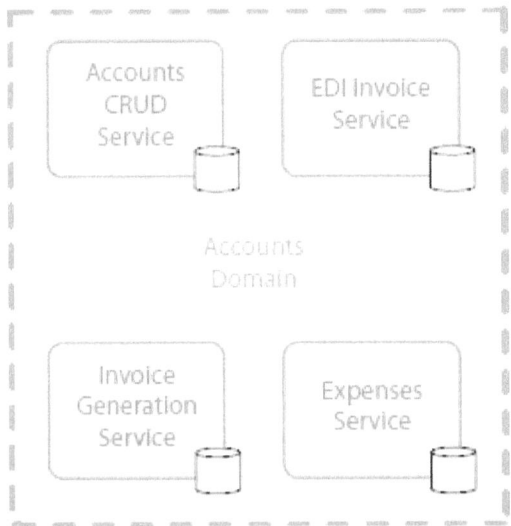

When splitting our microservices, we also need to remember that we can split microservices in order to have microservices just for data, in order to create, retrieve, update and delete data, and/or we can have microservices which specifically carry out a specific function, a business function. We must also be ready to fix incorrect boundaries, so, for example, if you have a microservice which needs to be split further, you must be ready to split that microservice. On the same hand, if you have two microservices which are more or less doing the same function, you should be comfortable with the fact that you can merge two microservices into one microservice. And when splitting our system into microservices, we also need to think about the inputs and outputs for each microservice, because this is the explicit interface of the microservice to the outside world, and later on these are the contracts that exist between our microservices. Sometimes we may need to split our system by technical boundaries. This might be because we need a special microservice, for example, to access archive data. Or we might need a special microservice in order to improve performance in a specific area. So overall, our microservices should business functions or business domains within the organization, but sometimes there might be exceptions where you've got a microservice for some kind of technical reason.

# Resilience

- Design for known failures
- Failure of downstream systems

  - Other services internal or external

- Degrade functionality on failure detection
- Default functionality on failure detection
- Design system to fail fast

  - Use timeouts
  - Use for connected systems
  - Timeout our requests after a threshold
  - Service to service
  - Service to other systems
  - Standard timeout length

- Adjust length on a case by case basis

- Network outages and latency
- Monitor timeouts
- Log timeouts

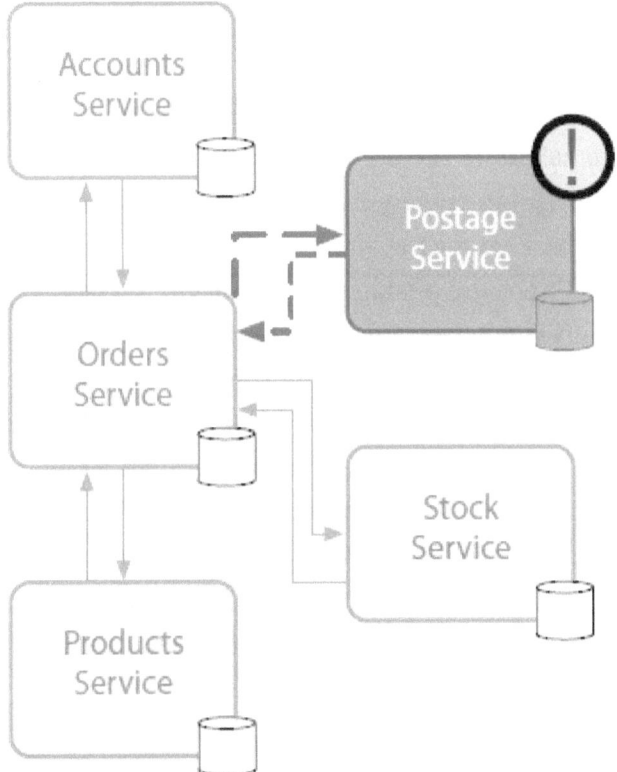

Another key design principle for microservices is resilience, especially when in a microservices architecture we have so many moving parts, and if one specific microservice failed, we can't have the entire system going down because of one failure. So during the design stage of our microservice, we need to design our microservice for all known failures. The next question is, what failures are known to us? The known failures are basically failures of downstream systems, systems which basically our microservice relies on in order to carry out a specific task. These might be internal services or external services, so for example, in our diagram we have our Orders Service which relies on the Postage Service in order to calculate the postage for an order. So at the design stage we question, what happens if the Postage Service goes down and we can't get the postage rate from the service? This is where we need to design our Order Service to either degrade functionality on failure detection or to default functionality on failure detection. So in our system when someone is placing an order and the Postage Service goes down, we might choose not to display the postage costs, and instead display a warning that postage at this stage cannot be displayed. We basically degrade the functionality of the system, or we can default the functionality. So instead of using the postage rate from the postage service, we instead use a standard rate, basically default the functionality. So when we design our system to handle failure, another thing we need to do is to design our system so that it fails fast, because there is no point to degrading functionality or defaulting functionality if our transaction takes a lot longer to complete. A hanging transaction or a delayed transaction might be as bad as seeing an error on the screen, so instead we need the system to fail fast and recover fast so as far as the user is concerned nothing has actually happened, and in order to fail fast, within our system we need to use timeouts. Timeouts are commonly used between connected systems. Timeouts basically allow us to say, if something doesn't respond within the given time, assume that they have failed. They basically allow us to timeout our requests after a certain threshold. So, for example, in our Postage Service example, if we have a timeout of 5 seconds, if the Postage Service doesn't reply within those 5 seconds, we know the Postage service is down, and therefore we can fail fast. We can then quickly degrade or default our functionality. We should try and use timeout functionality everywhere between service to service communication and service to other systems communication, and we also should specify a standard timeout length for our overall system, so the standard timeout length between services to services and services to other systems, and we should only adjust the timeout length between two systems if there is an exception, but we should try and use our standard timeout length throughout our system. Remember, timeouts will not only help with downstream systems going down, but it will also help with network outages and network latencies. Network issues is also another type of failure, and luckily for us, timeouts can be used to cater both for network issues and for downstream systems coming down. In that system we should also continuously monitor our timeouts and log our timeouts. This will help us see that within our system we have downstream systems that are not always responding or we have the occasional network issues. It makes all our issues transparent if we are monitoring our timeouts and logging them. So not only will monitoring timeouts and logging timeouts make our system health more transparent, but long-term when it comes to problem solving any specific behaviors of our system, logging timeouts will help us workout if specific behaviors are related to timeout issues. In the next two sections of the module, we will look at monitoring and logging

## Observable : Centralized Monitoring

- Centralized monitoring
- Real-time monitoring
- Monitor the host

- CPU, memory, disk usage, etc.

- Expose metrics within the services

    - Response times
    - Timeouts
    - Exceptions and errors

- Business data related metrics

    - Number of orders
    - Average time from basket to checkout

- Collect and aggregate monitoring data

    - Monitoring tools that provide aggregation
    - Monitoring tools that provide drill down options

- Monitoring tool that can help visualise trends
- Monitoring tool that can compare data across servers
- Monitoring tool that can trigger alerts

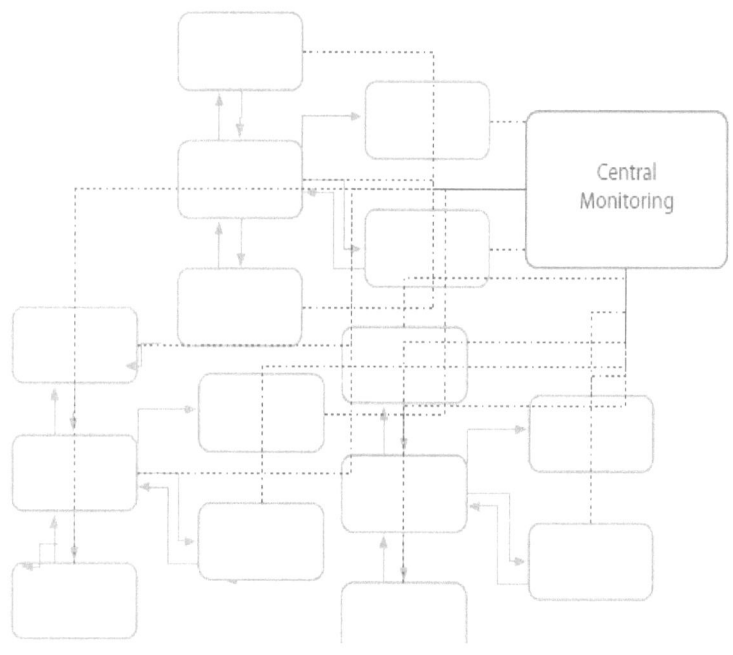

Another key design principle for microservices architecture is that our microservices are observable. In the microservices architecture, our system will consist of multiple microservices and multiple instances of microservices, therefore, it's important that we can see the system health in a transparent way, and one way of doing this is to have a centralized monitoring system within your architecture, something that produces monitoring data in real time so as soon as there's an issue you can start seeing this issue in your centralized monitoring system. And you need to monitor the health of the host, which runs your service in terms of CPU usage, memory usage, and disk usage, and you also need to monitor the service itself, and you can do that by exposing metrics within your service, things like response times, so the time it takes for a service to reply to your service. You also need to monitor things like timeouts, so if a service doesn't respond within a given amount of time and therefore it has failed to serve your service, you need to log this in your monitoring system, as well as monitoring the number of timeout errors. You should also monitor the number of exceptions or errors that happen across your microservices. Basically monitor anything that indicates the current health of the system. You can also expand your central monitoring system to include business data related metrics, for example, the number of orders you've currently taken, or the average time from basket to checkout. We need a central monitoring tool that not only collects data, but also aggregates that monitoring data, so at a high level we can see trends and history with the options to drill down into the detail, if required. We also need a monitoring tool to be able to visualize trends so that we can see patterns and spot potential problems. We also need our monitoring tool to have the ability to compare data across servers, because our microservices will live on multiple servers, and therefore the ability to compare data for different servers is key. We also need a monitoring tool to have the ability to trigger alerts if one of our specific measures exceeds a threshold. So, for example, on a given day if our central monitoring tool detects the fact that we've had more than one timeout during the day, it might send an alert to all interested parties so that they can react and fix the issue. In the next section of the module, we will look at how centralized logging can be used to make our microservices architecture more observable.

## Observable: Centralized Logging

- Centralized Logging
  - When to log
    - Startup or shutdown
    - Code path milestones
      - Requests, responses and decisions
    - Timeouts, exceptions and errors
  - Structured logging

- Level

  - Information
  - Error
  - Debug
  - Statistic

- Date and time
- Correlation ID
- Host name
- Service name and service instance
- Message

- Traceable distributed transactions

  - Correlation ID

    - Passed service to service

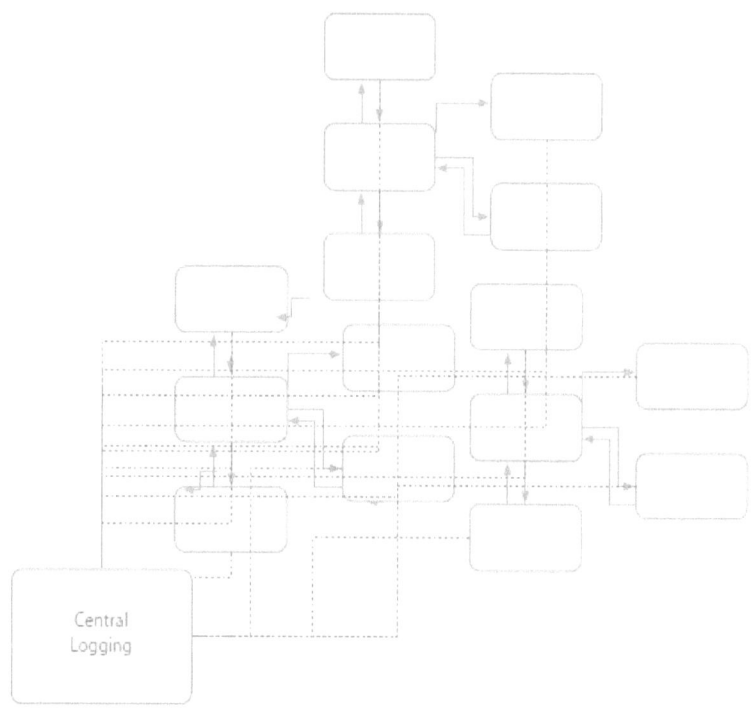

Another way to make our microservices more observable is to have centralized logging. The difference between centralized logging and centralized monitoring is when we are monitoring we are collecting numbers and counts, i.e., measures. When we are logging, we are actually recording information, detailed information about events, and because they record detailed information about events, they tell a story. They allow us to see what's happened, why it happened, and how it happened. And in a complex microservices architecture where you have multiple microservices and multiple instances of microservices, this kind of information is key for problem solving, and especially when most transactions within this type of system are distributed transactions, we need a way, a centralized way of seeing the whole story, the life story, of a transaction. And it's key to create these log entries when our microservices start up or when our microservices shut down, and it's also key to create these log entries when there are code path milestones, for example, when you receive requests or when you make responses, or when you make decisions within the code, only key milestones which will help us problem solve later on. We also need to treat timeouts, exceptions, and errors as events that we need to log. The information we record regarding a specific event should also be structured, and that structure should be consistent across our system. So, for example, our structured log entry might contain level information to state if the log entry is for information, or it's information regarding an error, or it's debug information, or it's statistics that's been recorded as a log entry event. The structured log entry must also have a date and a time so we know when the event happened. We should also include a correlation ID in our structured logging so that we can trace distributed transactions across our logs. We should also include the host name within our structured log so that we know exactly where the log entry came from. We should also include the service name and the service instance so we know exactly which microservice made the log entry. And finally, we should also include a message in our structured logging which is the key information which is associated with the event. So, for example, for an error this might be the CallStack or details regarding the exception. The key thing is, we keep our structured logging format consistent. A consistent format will allow us to query the logging information. We can basically then search for specific patterns and specific issues using our centralized logging tool. Another key aspect of centralized logging within a microservices architecture is to make distributed transactions more traceable. We briefly mentioned the idea of a correlation ID. A correlation ID is a unique ID which is assigned to every transaction, so when the transaction becomes distributed across services we can follow that transaction across our services using logging information. The correlation ID is basically passed from service to service. Basically all services that process that specific transaction receive that correlation ID so that they can log any events associated with that transaction to our centralized logs. In the next section of the module, we will be looking at the automation design principle for microservices.

## Automation: CI Tools

- Continuous Integration Tools
    - Work with source control systems
    - Automatic after check-in
    - Unit tests and integration tests required
    - Ensure quality of check-in
        - Code compiles
        - Tests pass
        - Changes integrate
        - Quick feedback
    - Urgency to fix quickly
    - Creation of build
    - Build ready for test team
    - Build ready for deployment

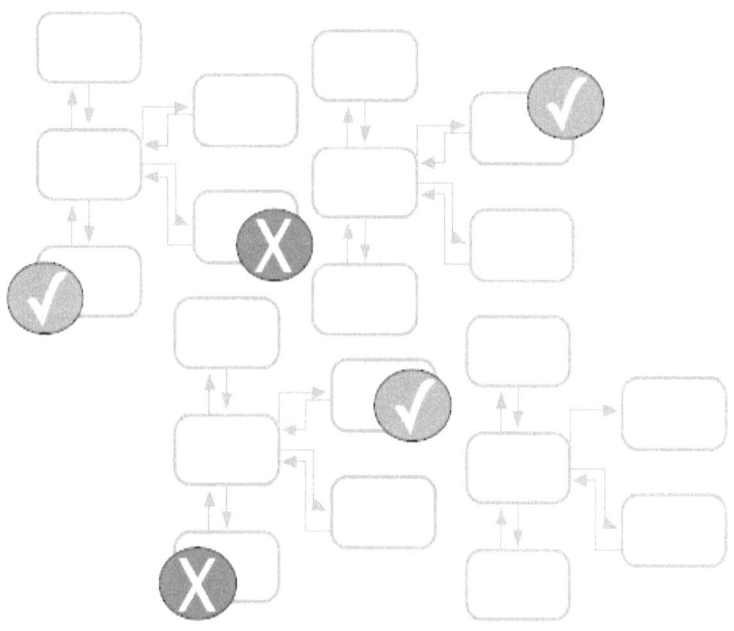

Another key design principle for microservices architecture is automation. One aspect of automation in the microservices context is the use of tools to provide automatic testing and feedback for software changes. These tools are normally known as Continuous Integration Tools, and these Continuous Integration Tools basically work with our source control system. They automatically test our software after we check-in and change to the software into the source control system where they test our software by basically running unit tests and integration tests that we've written. Unit tests and integration tests are basically bits of code which is designed to test our production code. They basically test that a change or enhancement in the code doesn't break any of the existing requirements. So in order to fully benefit from using continuous integration tools, unit tests and integration tests should be implemented, so continuous integration tools basically allow us to ensure that our code compiles, and that our tests pass, and that our changed software integrates with anything else that might use our software, and these tools also provide us with quick feedback. So if a change to a microservice breaks the microservice itself, or breaks anything else which might use a microservice, the Continuous Integration Tool will give us quick feedback so that we can fix the issue quickly. So in a microservices system with so many moving parts, this kind of information on the quality of integration is super useful. Quick feedback also causes an urgency to fix things quickly and issues don't pile up, because automatic feedback is sent to the team and then can quickly address the issue. In fact, the team culture should be to stop any development until all issues reported by the Continuous Integration Tool have been fixed. The continuous integration tool can also be used to build our software as part of the test, and this build can be used by the test team to test the software, and it can also be used for deployment. In the next section of the module, we'll look at how deployment tools can be used to take builds created by the Continuous Integration Tools and have them deployed automatically.

## Automation: CD Tools

- Continuous Deployment Tools
    - Automate software deployment
        - Configure once
        - Works with CI tools
        - Deployable after check in
        - Reliably released at anytime
    - Benefits
        - Quick to market
        - Reliable deployment
        - Better customer experience

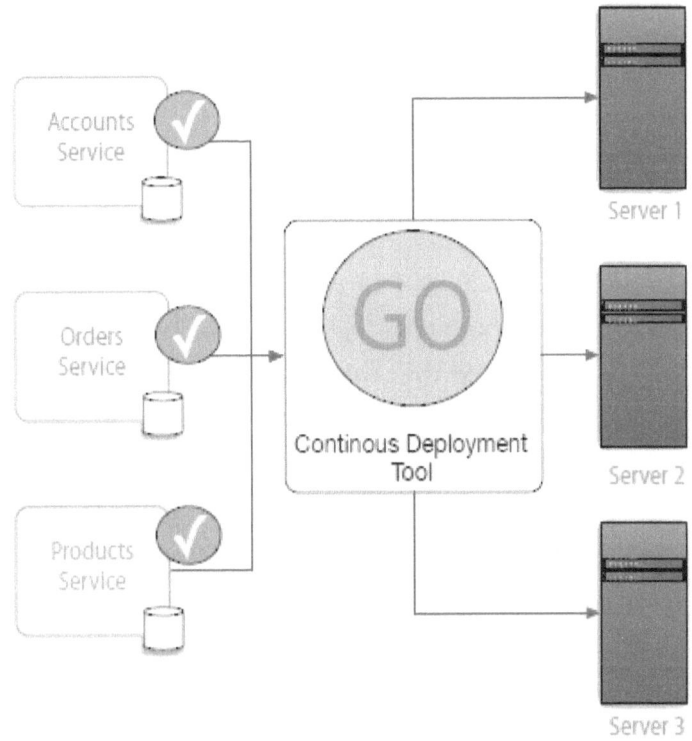

Another aspect of automation when it comes to microservices is the use of automatic deployment tools, and they are known as Continuous Deployment Tools, and they basically automate our software deployment, and in a microservices system where you might have multiple microservices and multiple instances on different servers, on a number of different servers, this type of software is super useful. Initially you have to take time out to configure the tool so the tool knows exactly what software to take from where, and where to place the software, and how to configure the software in the target location, however, this configuration is only required once, and the configuration is reused on future releases. So when a new version of your software is available, you can use the same configuration to re-deploy it again automatically, and this type of deployment tool normally works with a Continuous Integration Tool, which creates the build that this tool will deploy. And as long as all the continuous integration tests pass, the new version of the software is deployable after checking once the tests have passed. As long as your production environment does not physically change, Continuous Deployment Tools can be used at any time to reliably release your software into production. They can be configured to upgrade websites, web services, to upgrade databases, so when you are developing your microservices, ensure that Continuous Deployment Tools are part of the plan. Continuous Deployment Tools can also give your company a competitive edge because you can get new versions of your software out to the market very quickly and in a reliable way. And because of reliable deployment, the customer will also have a better experience. So when designing your microservices, you need to keep in mind what the end deployment configuration for your microservice will be, because we need to translate this configuration into our Continuous Deployment Tool.

## Module Summary

- High Cohesion
    - Single thing done well
    - Single focus
- Approach
    - Keeps splitting service until it only has one reason to change
- Autonomous
    - Independently changeable and deployable
- Approach
    - Loosely coupled system
    - Versioning strategy
    - Microservice ownership by team
- Business Domain Centric
    - Represent business function or represent a business domain
- Approach
    - Course grain business domains

- Subgroup into functions and areas

- Resilience
  - Embrace Failure
  - Default or degrade functionality

- Approach
  - Design for known failures
  - Fail fast and recover fast
- Observable
  - See system health
  - Centralized logging and monitoring

- Approach
  - Tools for real-time centralized monitoring
  - Tools for centralized structured logging

- Automation
  - Tools for testing and feedback
  - Tools for deployment
- Approach
  - Continuous Integration Tools
  - Continuous Deployment Tools

In this module, we learned the design approaches we can take in order to implement the design principles of the microservices architecture. In order for our microservices to have high cohesion, we must keep splitting our microservices until they have only one reason to change. We also learned in order to make our microservices autonomous, our system should be loosely coupled, and that we should have a versioning strategy to ensure that our microservices are always backwards compatible. We also learned, in order to make microservices more autonomous, i.e., independently changeable and deployable, it's best if the ownership of a microservice is given to a team so that they can ensure that the microservice is designed to be independently changeable and deployable. We also learned, in order to make microservices business domain centric we must first define our microservices as coarse grain business domains. We then further subgroup them into functions and areas, i.e., further divide them into microservices to present those functions and areas. We also learned in order to make our microservices more resilient we must design them for known failures and we must design them in a way where they fail fast and recover fast. We also learned in order to make our microservices more observable, so that the system health is more transparent, we should use tools for real-time centralized monitoring and tools for centralized structured logging. We also learned the fact that in order to introduce automation into a microservices architecture, in order to speed up testing and deployment, we should use Continuous Integration Tools and Continuous Deployment Tools. In the next module, we'll look at the technology that's available to make all of this possible.

# Module 3 : Technology for Microservices

## Introduction

- Module Overview
  - Communication
  - Hosting Platforms
  - Observable Microservices
  - Performance
  - Automation Tools

In this module we will look at technologies that help us enable a microservices architecture. We'll look at communication technologies for microservices, and we'll look at hosting platforms for microservices, and we'll also look at technologies that make microservices observable. We'll then move on to looking at technologies that help with performance, and then we conclude the module by looking at automation tools.

## Communication: Synchronous

- Request response communication
  - Client to service
  - Service to service
  - Service to external
- Remote procedure call
  - Sensitive to change
- HTTP
  - Work across the internet
  - Firewall friendly
- REST
  - CRUD using HTTP verbs
  - Natural decoupling
  - Open communication protocol
  - REST with HATEOS
- Synchronous issues
  - Both parties have to be available.
  - Performance subject to network quality

- Client must know the location of service(host/port)

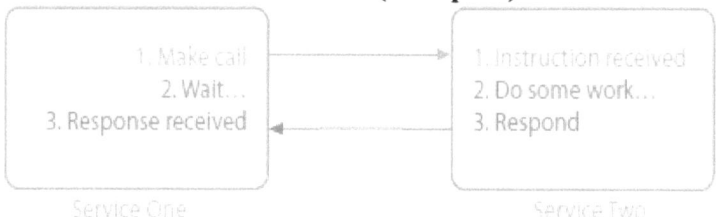

In this section of the module we will look at communication technologies that can be used for microservices. We will look at synchronous communication technologies and we will look at asynchronous communication technologies. So when using synchronous communication between our microservices, we basically make requests and then wait for responses, and this kind of communication can happen between our client applications and our services, or between service to service communication, or between a service and an external system. So in our example here, Service One makes a call to Service Two, and then Service Two receives that request as an instruction, and then based on that instruction Service Two carries out some work, and then once that work is complete Service Two responds to Service One. And as you can see, this communication is synchronous because when Service One makes a call to Service Two, it has to wait for Service Two to complete its work before it will actually receive a response.

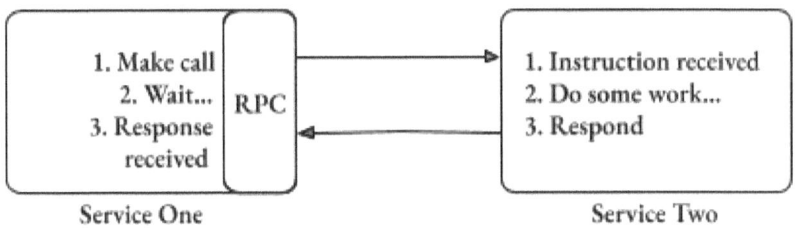

One of the technology types that can be used to make this kind of communication is called remote procedure call. Remote procedure call implementations basically allow you to create distributed client server programs, and remote procedure call libraries normally hide the fact that you're communicating and making calls over a network, and when coding remote procedure calls it's almost like coding a call to an internal method. Within the client itself, the remote procedure call libraries basically shield all the detail regarding the network protocols and the communication protocols. It appears as if you're making a call to a local function or method, but in fact you're actually calling a remote method or function on a remote service. However, the problem with RPC is that it's sensitive to change, any changes at the server end. So in our example, if we change Service Two it will mean that Service One will break. Changes like changing the method signatures at the server end will break all client applications. Another technology that can be used for request response synchronous communication is HTTP.

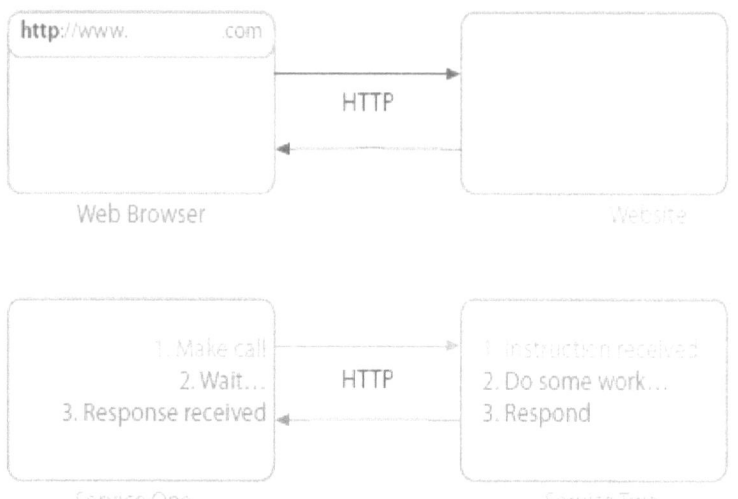

HTTP is a communication protocol that we're used to using over the web, so when you request pages in a web browser it's basically using HTTP communication in order to talk to the web server and retrieve the work page, and this same communication protocol can be used between microservices to make request response synchronous communication calls. And because it works over the web, it's also firewall friendly. It's basically a communication protocol that network architectures are used to dealing with because it's used over the internet, and therefore, things like firewalls can be configured quite easily to let HTTP traffic through. You can even have RPC calls that are made using HTTP.

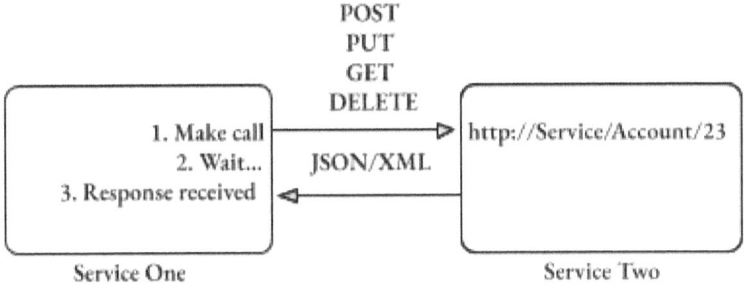

Another type of communication protocol that can be used over HTTP to provide request response synchronous communication is REST, and when using REST, the entities within our system can basically be accessed using endpoint URLs which basically map to our entities within our system. In this example, I'm using an endpoint to retrieve an account record with an ID of 23 from Service Two by using this URL. Not only can I retrieve records, but I can also create, retrieve, update, and delete records using HTTP verbs, POST, PUT, GET, and DELETE, which basically map to CRUD operations. So in our account example I can actually create an account using POST, and I can update an account using PUT, and I can retrieve an account using GET, and I can also delete an account using DELETE. REST also provides natural decoupling, because the data returned is always in JSON or XML format, which is normally different to the internal representation of that entity. REST is also an open communication protocol in that it doesn't dictate what technology is either used at the client end or at the server end, both the natural decoupling and open communication protocol characteristics of REST make it ideal for microservices. Another key feature of REST that can be used is called HATEOS. This is basically a technique of including links to related resources in responses you receive. So, for example, if I use an HTTP POST call to create an account, the response I'll get from Service Two will include a link to the newly-created account so that I can use HTTP GET in order to retrieve that account using that link provided. And in a microservices architecture this is ideal, because this means that communication will be less chatty and therefore even more decoupled, because the communication we do make will result in responses that includes extra information, and that will help us work with related entities. The main issues with synchronous communication are that both parties have to be available during the communication. Service One basically has to wait for Service Two to respond before Service One can carry on doing other stuff, and in a microservices architecture we have distributed transactions using many services. A slow-down in one service could slow the entire transaction down. It also makes the performance of our system and our transactions subject to the network quality, because it might not be the service that's running slowly, it might be that the network is running slowly, therefore, responses from services arrive slowly. The other problem we have with synchronous communication is because the service talks directly to another service or system, it must know the location of that service. However, this problem can be resolved by using service registration and discovery patterns, as well as other components on the network like load balancers. In the next section of the module we will look at asynchronous communication and how asynchronous communication can be used to avoid some of the problems associated with synchronous communication.

## Asynchronous Communication

- Event based
  - Mitigates the need of client and service availability
  - Decouples client and service
- Message queueing protocol
  - Message Brokers

        - Subscriber and publisher are decoupled
        - Microsoft message queuing (MSMQ)
        - RabbitMQ
        - ATOM (HTTP to propagate events)
    - Asynchronous challenge
        - Complicated
        - Reliance on message broker
        - Visibility of the transaction
        - Managing the messaging queue
    - Real world systems
        - Would use both synchronous and asynchronous

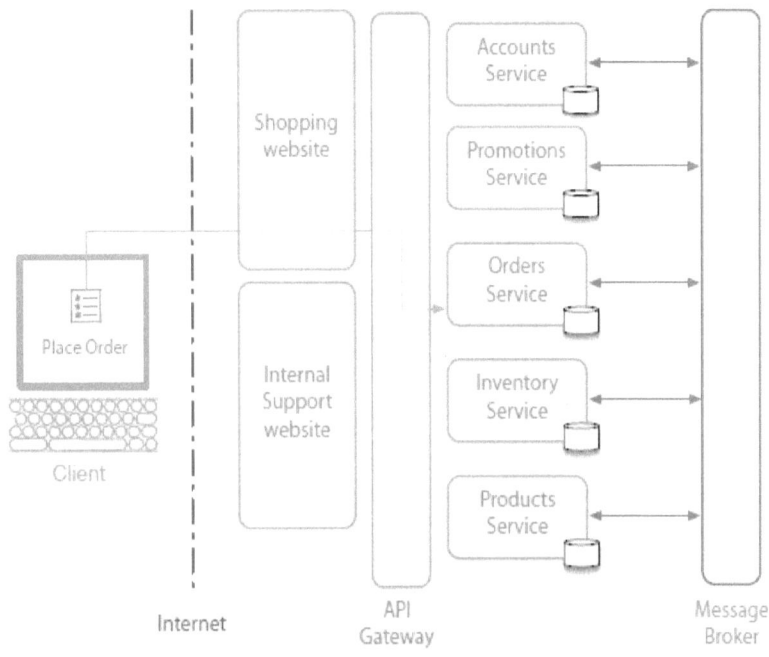

In this section of the module, we will look at how asynchronous communication can be used with microservices. So asynchronous communication in a microservices context basically means event-based communication. So when our service needs another service to carry out a task, instead of connecting directly to that service, the service basically creates an event, and services that can carry that task out will automatically pick that event up, and therefore, in this type of event-based asynchronous communication, there is no need for the client and the server to connect. It basically decouples the client and the service, and this type of communication normally uses a message queuing protocol where the events created by a service are seen as messages, where the service creating these messages is seen as a publisher, and the service which carries out tasks in response to to these messages is seen as a subscriber. And these messages are normally stored and buffered by a message broker until a subscriber picks these messages up and the subscriber and the publisher only actually know of the message broker, and therefore they're decoupled from each other, and therefore, the subscriber and the publisher also don't need to know each other's location. And in a microservices architecture, this kind of communication protocol will be perfect because we can spawn up new versions of microservices and new instances of microservices, and there's no need for each of them to know each others' location because they all communicate using a message queuing protocol. You can also have multiple subscribers acting on the same message. For example, in a microservices system you might have a service which has just recently changed the type of data and it needs to inform all other services to refresh the cache for that data. We also have many vendors that provide message queuing protocols. We have Microsoft with Microsoft message queuing, and we have RabbitMQ, and we also have ATOM, which uses HTTP to propagate events. The problem with event-based asynchronous communication is that it's complicated, especially when you're using distributed transactions and you're using events in order to complete a distributed transaction. Another problem is, your system relies on a message broker. This is another additional component within the system that your system relies on, and another potential point of failure. Visibility of transactions can also be a problem. So not only are your transactions distributed, but the transactions are not completing in a synchronous way. You'll also need to learn new tools and techniques to manage the messaging queue. You will need to ensure the messaging queue is handled properly, and that the performance of the system is not affected if you have any queuing issues. You will find in a microservices system you will end up using both synchronous communication and asynchronous communication. In the next section of the module, we'll look at how we can host our microservices.

# Hosting Platforms : Virtualization | Containers | Self Hosting | Registry and Discovery

## Hosting Platforms: Virtualization

- A virtual machine as a host
- Foundation of cloud platforms
  - Platform as a service (PAAS)
    - Microsoft Azure
    - Amazon web services
    - Your own cloud (for example vSphere)
  - Could be more efficient
    - Takes time to setup
    - Takes time to load
    - Take quite a bit of resource
  - Unique features
    - Take snapshot
    - Clone instances
  - Standardised and mature

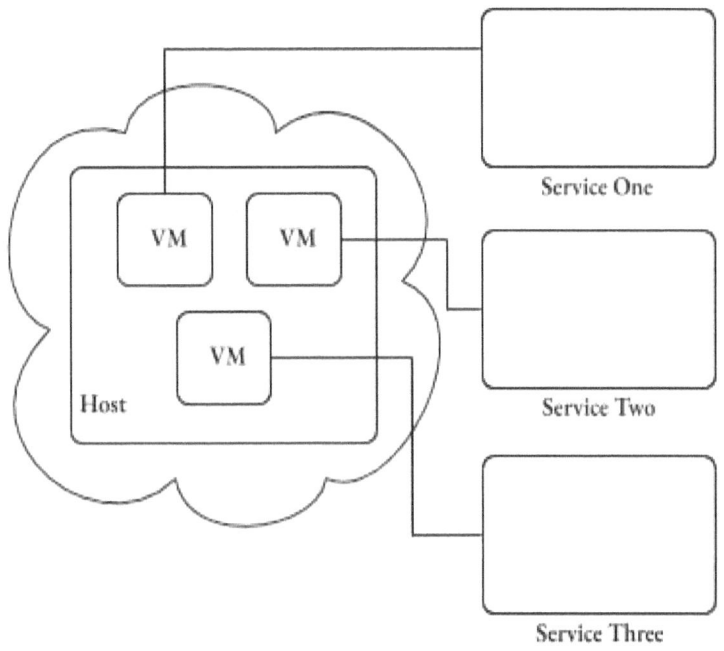

In this section of the module, we will look at how we can host our microservices. We will look at how virtualization can be used to host our microservices, and how containers can be used, and also how you can self-host your own microservices. We'll also look at how there's a need to register and discover microservices when hosting them. So one way of hosting microservices is to use virtualization. This is basically using virtual machines as a host in order to run the microservice. You no longer need to run your microservices on physical machines, instead you can just spin up a virtual machine, and install your microservice, and you've got self-contained machine that's running your microservice. Virtual machines are basically entire instances of operating systems running on hardware which is simulated in software, and therefore, on one physical machine you can have multiple virtual machines running, which act and behave as if they are physical machines themselves. The beauty of virtual machines is that you can clone them. So once you have your one virtual machine set up and you have your microservice installed, if you need multiple instances of that microservice, you can basically clone multiple copies of that virtual machine, and that's why virtual machines have been the foundation of many cloud platforms. You can now, in fact, subscribe to cloud platform services and these types of services are known as Platform as a service, and these types of services can provide you an entire infrastructure through cloud services in order to run your microservices architecture. You could run your entire microservices architecture in the cloud with vendors like Microsoft, who have an Azure platform, and vendors like Amazon who provide Amazon web services without actually owning a physical server. You could renew entire architecture in these cloud services, and within these services you could have multiple virtual machines running your complete architecture, and as the demand increases for your microservices, you could spin up extra virtual machines in order to run extra instances of your microservices. There are also platforms out there which allow you to create your own cloud, a cloud that you host yourself, a cloud which is basically made up of virtual machines in order to create an infrastructure, but it's a cloud that you host on your own physical machines. The only downside of virtual machines is that they could be more efficient. They can take a lot of time to set up and they can take some time to load, and they also can take quite a bit of resource. You have to remember these are entire instances of operating systems running in software-simulated hardware on top of another operating system. They do, however, have some unique features. You can, for example, take a snapshot of a virtual machine, and then at a later date you can restore that virtual machine back to the time when the snapshot was taken. We've already mentioned you can clone virtual machines. You could clone virtual machines that already have microservices running in them, and therefore, quickly creating multiple instances of that microservice when the demand for that microservice increases. The other good thing about virtualization is that the technology itself is now standardized and it's very mature. There are plenty of virtualization platforms available now with real good tooling. It's a very common thing these days to have your entire enterprise software running in a virtualized environment. In the next section of the module, we'll look at another virtualization technology which is slightly different to virtual machines. We will look at the Container technology.

## Hosting Platforms: Containers

- Type of virtualization
- Isolate services from each other
- Single service per container
- Different to a virtual machine
  - Use less resource than VM
  - Faster than VM
  - Quicker to create new instances
- Future of hosted apps
- Cloud platform support growing
- Mainly Linux based
- Not as established as virtual machines
  - Not standardised
  - Limited features and tooling

- - Infrastructure support in its infancy
  - Complex to setup
- Examples

  - Docker
  - Rocker
  - Glassware

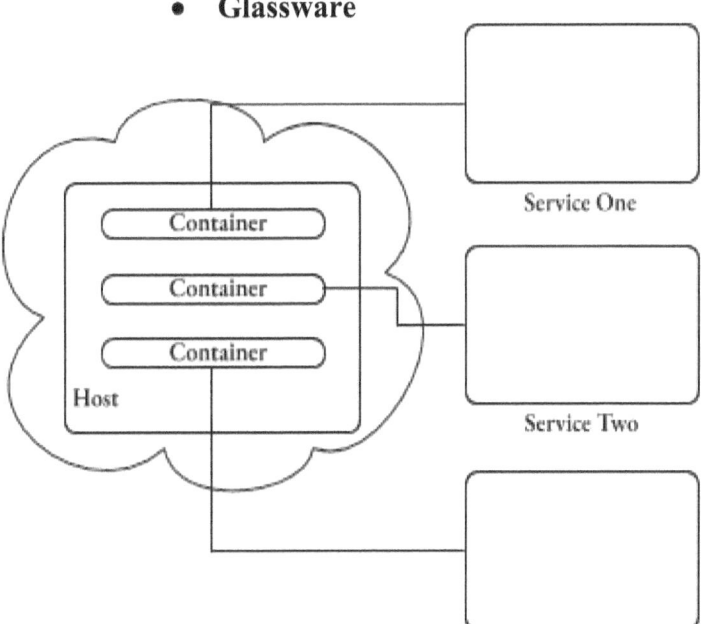

Another hosting option for microservices is the use of Containers. And containers are another type of virtualization, however, unlike virtual machines, they do not run an entire operating system within the container, they run the minimal amount required to run your service. They are a good way of isolating services from each other so that each service is more stable and more secure.

It's also a common practice to only run one service, one microservice, within a container. We've already mentioned the fact that they are different to virtual machines in that they don't contain an entire operating system, instead they have the minimal to run a microservice, and therefore, they use less resource than a virtual machine. This is resource in the form of CPU usage, memory usage, and disk usage from the host machine, and therefore, you can probably have many more containers running on a host machine than you can virtual machines running on a host machine. Containers also tend to run faster than virtual machines, and they tend to boot up a lot faster than virtual machines. And because containers are so lightweight and fast, it's quicker to create new instances to meet demand. And because of these characteristics, containers are also seen in the future of hosted applications, and cloud platform support for them is growing, so support from the likes of Azure and Amazon Web Services is growing. Currently containers are only Linux-based, but in the future Windows support is on the horizon. As a technology, they're also not quite yet established as virtual machine technology. The technology for containers isn't quite standardized yet, and there are limited features and tooling support. Infrastructure support is also in its infancy, and they're quite complex to set up when compared to virtual machines. Over time, container technology will standardize, and in the future they will play a key part in microservices architecture. Examples of container technology are Docker, Rocker, and Glassware. In the next section of the module, we will look at what it means to self-host microservices.

## Hosting Platforms: Self Hosting

- Implement your own cloud
    - Virtualization platform
    - Implement containers
- Use of physical machines
    - Single service on a server
    - Multiple services on a server
- Challenges
    - Long-term maintenance
    - Need for technicians
    - Training
    - Need for space
    - Scaling is not as immediate

In this section of the module, we will look at self-hosting as an option for implementing your microservices architecture. If you already have a good IT infrastructure and IT staff, self-hosting might be your primary option. Cloud-hosting services can make the implementation of a microservices architecture a lot simpler because you control the whole thing via a portal and there's no need for physical machines or specialized staff members in order to carry out specific tasks, but if you already have a good IT infrastructure, you might choose to implement your own cloud. You might implement your own virtualization platform or implement your own containers. If the implementation of these technologies is too complex to start off with, you can always start off by implementing your microservices architecture initially using physical machines where you have a single service on a server or multiple services on a server, however, long-term if you want to reap the full benefits of using a microservices architecture, you will end up using some kind of cloud technology so that you can at least scale up the system on demand. However, if you choose to implement the cloud platform yourself and have a local cloud instead of using an external cloud service like Microsoft Azure, there are some challenges. You'll have to think about the long-term maintenance of a cloud platform and the need for technicians, technicians that specialize in supporting cloud platform, and you'll also have to train your existing staff, and you'll probably need extra space for extra servers that you'll need to purchase in order to host the cloud platform. You still might find that scaling is not as immediate as buying an external service, because in order to scale up your cloud services you still have to buy the physical machines. In the next section of the module, we'll look at how, when you do scale up your system by creating new instances of microservices, how those microservices register themselves, and how clients can discover them.

## Hosting Platforms: Registration and Discovery

- Where?
- Host, port and version
- Service registry database
- Register on startup
- Deregister service on failure

- Cloud platforms make it easy
- Local platform registration options
  - Self registration
  - Third-party registration
- Local platform discovery options
  - Client-side discovery
  - Server-side discovery

Now we will look at registry and discovery of microservices within your architecture. So, basically, when you create new instances of a microservice because you're scaling up, how is your system aware that that microservice is now available to carry out work? So when we need to connect to a microservice, we need to know where that microservice is, i.e., what host the microservice is running on, and what port it's listening on, and the version of that microservice. One way of storing this information and making this data available to your system is by having a service registry database. So when you implement new microservices or when you create new instances of microservices to meet demand, on startup these microservices register themselves on this database. You could even make your system clever enough so that when a microservice stops responding, the system deregisters that instance of the microservice from the service registry database. This makes the system almost kind of self-heal. New client requests will not connect to the microservice instance that's experiencing problems. Service registration and service deregistration are only really an issue when you're hosting the microservices yourself. Cloud services like Amazon Web Services or Microsoft Azure can make service registration or service deregistration quite straightforward and automatic. So in your self-hosted system, how can these microservices register themselves in this service registry database? Option 1 is they register themselves on startup, or you can have a third party piece of software which detects new instances of microservices and registers them on the registry database. Now that all your services are registered in a service registry database, how do the clients learn of all the locations? The options are, the clients either directly connect to the service registry database in order to learn the location of specific instances of microservices or you use some kind of gateway which all the clients connect to, and it's the gateway that retrieves the location from the service registry database. The process of a client connecting to the service registry database in order to find the location of a specific microservice, is known as client-side discovery. When a gateway or a load balancer or a similar type of component is instead used to connect to the service registry database on behalf of the client in order to find the location of a microservice, this process is known as server-side discovery.

## Observable Microservices: Monitoring Tech | Logging Tech

## Observable Microservices: Monitoring Tech

| | |
|---|---|
| tools | - Centralised
- Nagios
- PRTG
- Load balancers
- New Relic
- Desired |
| features | - Metrics across servers
- Automatic or minimal configuration |

- Client libraries to send metrics
- Test transactions support
- Alerting
- Network monitoring
- Standardise monitoring
- Central tool
- Preconfigured virtual machines or containers
- Real-time monitoring

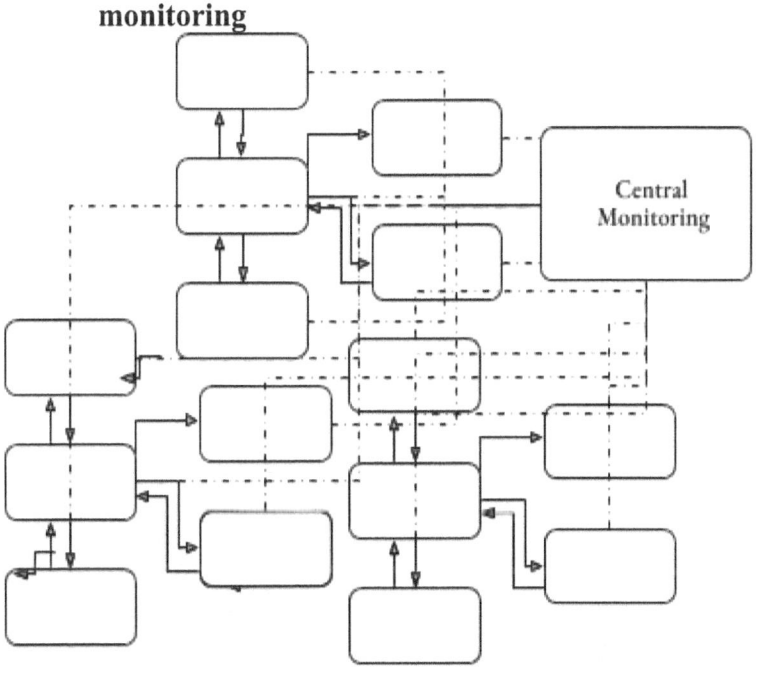

In this section of the module, we will look at monitoring technologies and logging technologies that make our microservices observable. In the previous module, we looked at why monitoring microservices is important, and the good news is there are a number of central monitoring tools out there. We have tools like Nagios, PRTG, and we even have some components within our system, like load balancers, that can also carry out some monitoring. There are also a number of online services, like New Relic, that can tap into your system and monitor it. The key features we recquire from our centralised monitoring tool is the ability to gather metrics across servers, and functionality to aggregate this data and to visualize this data. We also want a tool that provides automatic or minimal configuration, so that when we do create new instances of our microservices they automatically, or with minimal configuration, start being monitored. A tool that also allows the use of client libraries to send metrics will also be useful so that we can create custom client libraries that send data that we want to monitor. A monitoring tool that can send test transactions and monitor those test transactions is also useful. A monitoring tool that can also send alerts when something being monitored is not as expected is also useful. In a microservices system, the network is a key component, especially when most transactions are distributed transactions which make use of the network, so therefore, a monitoring tool that can also monitor the network is super useful. In our microservices architecture, we need to ensure that monitoring is standardised across the whole system, and this can be achieved by using a central tool and also by ensuring that all our hosts, our virtual machines and containers, are preconfigured with everything that's required in order for them to be monitored. We also need to ensure that monitoring is real-time, because in a complex architecture like a microservices architecture, if there's a problem, we need to know immediately so that we can react in a proactive manner. In the next section we will look at what technologies can be used for logging events that are happening within our system.

## Observable Microservices: Logging Tech

- Portal for centralised logging data
- Elastic log
- Log stash
- Splunk
- Kibana

| | |
|---|---|
| libraries | - Graphite
- Client logging
- Serilog
- and many more… |
| features | - Desired
- Structured logging
- Logging across servers
- Automatic or minimal configuration
- Correlation\Context ID for transactions |
| logging | - Standardise
- Central tool
- Template for client library |

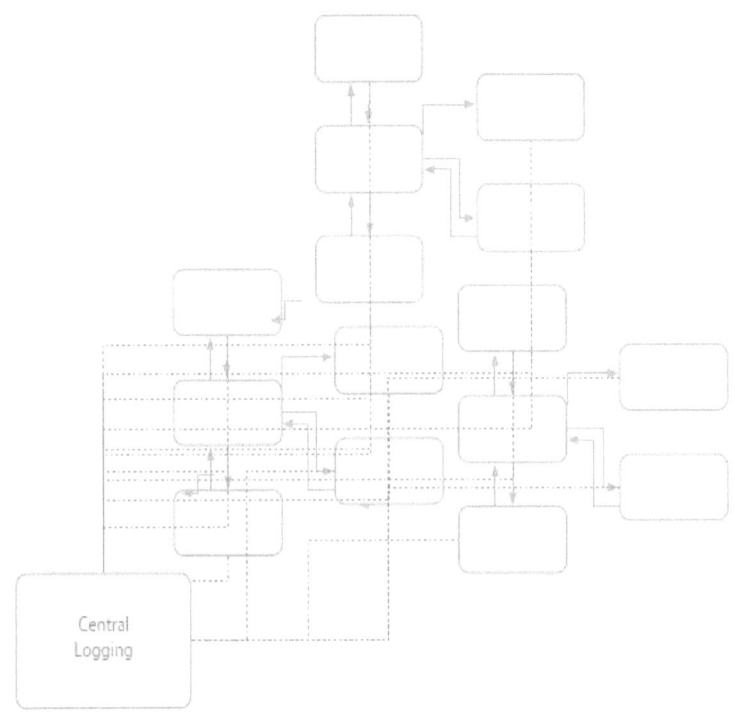

Now we will look at all the logging technology that's available to make our microservices observable. In the previous module, we looked at why logging was important for microservices, mainly why the logging of specific events within our system was important for problem solving. The good news is, there's a number of centralised tools which act as a portal for logging data. You basically push the logs at these tools, and then these tools basically store the logging data in a central database. So when a specific event happens within our system, we basically send the log to the centralised tools, and then the centralised tool will store all the data as a log entry into a database, and these centralised tools normally also provide a frontend which allows you to look at this logging data and also to query and find patterns within this logging data. So, for example, using the Correlation ID or the Transaction ID, I can look at the journey of our transaction through our system, through all the microservices it's gone through as a distributed transaction, by creating a query for that Transaction or Correlation ID within the centralised tool, and there are a number of centralised logging tools which provide all of these functionalities. Within the microservice itself, you also need to implement a client logging library which basically pushes the log against our centralised tool, and an example of this is something called Serilog. Serilog can be configured to push and raise events against our centralised logging tool, so that the log gets stored centrally. The desired features for both the client logging libraries and the centralised logging tool is that they support structured logging. We need our logs across the system to have structure so that they can be queried and they contain a minimal amount of information that's useful. And because our system is distributed with distributed transactions, we need our logging to work across servers. We need our centralised tool to have the ability to accept data from multiple servers, and we also need our centralised logging tool to be automatic or minimal in terms of configuration so that when we create new instances of our microservices because there's an increase in demand, our microservices can instantly start logging data to our centrlised tool. And because we are using distributed transactions within a microservices architecture, it's key that we can log a Correlation or a Context ID and that we can query a Correlation or a Context ID within our data. Across the system, we need to ensure that we standardise our logging, and we achieve this by using a central tool and also by providing a template for our client libraries that actually carry out the logging and pushing off the logs to the central tool, so that next time we create a new microservice we can take this template for the client logging library and implement it, and therefore, we can ensure that the format of the log, the structure of the log, is the same standard format used across the system.

# Microservices Performance: Scaling | Caching | API Gateway

## Microservices Performance: Scaling

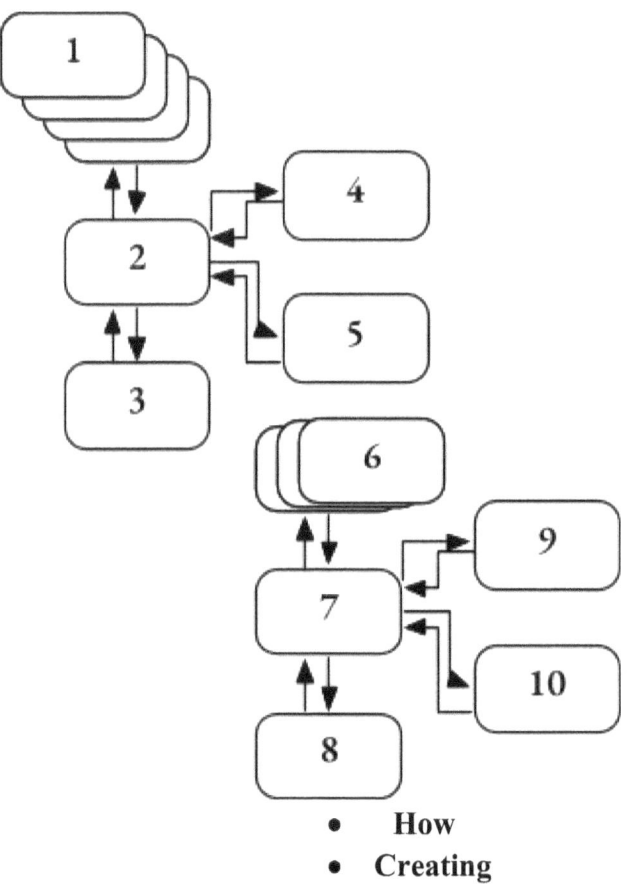

- How
- Creating multiple instances of service

- Adding resource to existing service

on-demand
- Automated or
- PAAS auto

scaling options
- Virtualization

and containers
- Physical host

servers
- Load balancers
- API Gateway
- When to scale

up
- Performance issues
- Monitoring data
- Capacity planning

In this section of the module, we'll look at how we can meet the performance requirements of our microservices by using scaling, caching, and API Gateways. So in a microservices system, when the performance requirements increase, or the performance degrades, we normally address this by scaling the system up, and this normally happens by increasing the number of instances of the microservice that's in demand or by adding extra resource to the host that's running a particular service. So this might be in the form of increasing the number of CPU calls that are available to a service, or the amount of memory that's available to a service, or the amount of disk or bandwidth that's available to a service. And the way you increase the number of instances of the service or the amount of resource available to a service might be automated or on-demand. With the automated option, the system will automatically detect that the system requires extra resource or extra instances of a particular service, and it will automatically increase the system in these areas. With the on-demand option, it might be as simple as logging onto a portal and increasing the number of instances for a service and adding extra resource, or the on-demand option might be as manual as adding extra hardware or software in order to meet the demand. Cloud-based services like Microsoft Azure and Amazon Web Services are know to provide auto scaling options, so when the demand increases, the system scales up in an automated way. Automated and on-demand scaling up is only possible because of technologies like virtualization and containers. Increasing the number of physical host servers in order to scale up is nowadays deemed as the slower option. Virtualization and containers are seen as a quick way of increasing the number of virtual hosts that are running our services. Once we've scaled up our system by increasing the number of instances of a particular service, the next thing we need is a load balancer, and this can be in the form of an API Gateway, something which basically takes in all the incoming requests for a service and then shares the requests between the instances of that service, i.e., balances the load across the system to improve performance. Later on we will also look at the other things an API Gateway can do as well as load balancing. So when do you scale up? You need to basically scale up when there are performance issues, or when your monitoring data shows that you will have performance issues, or when your capacity planning shows that there's going to be increase in usage in the future. It might be that automated scaling up can be configured to cover most of these scenarios. In the next section we will look at how caching can be used to improve our system's performance.

# Microservices Performance: Caching

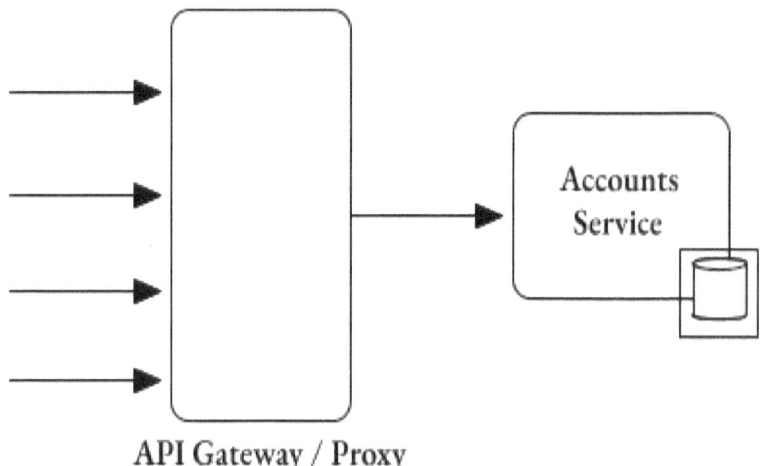

API Gateway / Proxy

- Caching to reduce
- Client calls to services
- Service calls to databases
- Service to service calls

- API Gateway\Proxy level
- Client side
- Service level
- Considerations
- Simple to setup and manage
- Data leaks

Another way to improve the performance of a microservices architectured system is to use caching, caching of data. Caching is a way of basically detecting that multiple calls are asking for the same thing, and instead of honoring each request you honor one request, retrieve the data, and then use the same data to satisfy all other requests, and therefore, caching improves performance by reducing the client calls to a service, service calls to a database, and service to service calls. The ideal place to implement caching within a microservices architectured system, is at the API Gateway level or at the proxy server level. This way the caching implementation is invisible to everything else, and at this level, not only will it reduce the number of calls to our services and our databases, but it will also reduce the amount of traffic within our network. Caching can also be done at the client-side level, for example, single page applications that download most of the data they need and work with that data until they need to make a call back to the system. You could also implement caching at service level, so when Service A equals Service B it caches the response from Service B, and Service A might be configured to only refresh that data once a day because it's static data. In terms of requirements, we want our caching system to be simple to set up and manage, because in a complex microservices architectured system, caching needs to be simple and easy to implement. Another concern to do with caching is data leaks. We do not want to accidentally present the wrong data to the wrong call. In the next section of the module, we will look at how API Gateways can help with improving microservices performance.

## Microservices Performance: API Gateway

performance
- Help with
- Load balancing
- Caching

- Help with
- Creating central entry point
- Exposing services to clients
- One interface to many services
- Dynamic location of services
- Routing to specific instance of service

- Service registry database
- Security
- API Gateway
- Dedicated security service
- Central security vs service level

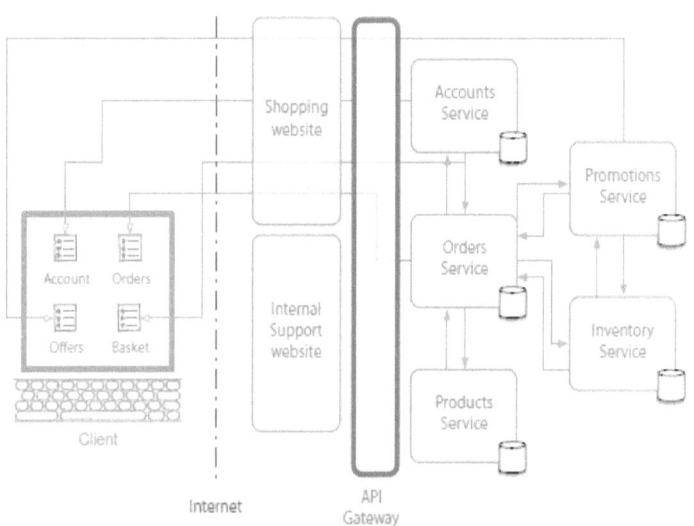

In this section of the module, we will look at how API Gateways can be used to improve microservices performance. So API Gateways are basically the central entry point into our system for client applications, and therefore, they can be used to improve performance by having load balancing functionality and by having caching functionality. And because they are the central point of entry, they simplify the implementation of load balancing and caching. The rest of the system can be oblivious to the fact that we have load balancing and caching implemented, that's what makes API Gateways so useful. So overall, API Gateways help with creating our central point into our system, and exposing our services to clients, and also they provide one interface to many services. In the background we could increase the number of microservices or move our microservices around in terms of location, but the client application won't realize, because their main entry point is the API Gateway, and it hides all the detail in terms of the location of the microservices within the system, so it helps with dynamic location of services. API Gateways can also be configured to route specific calls to a specific instance of a service. So, for example, all calls from European clients might be directed to instances of microservices which are located in Europe. They can also be configured to look up the location of microservices in a service registry database in order to help with load balancing. They can also be used to provide security for the overall system by providing authentication and authorization. They might have a dedicated service in the background which gives them all the data they need in terms of security, so having security built into the

API Gateway is a central way of implementing security, but you might choose to have security and authorization both at the API Gateway level, and at the individual service level. So as you can see, not only do API Gateways help with performance, but they can help simplify overall microservices architecture.

## Automation Tools: Continuous Integration | Continuous Deployment

# Automation Tools: Continuous Integration

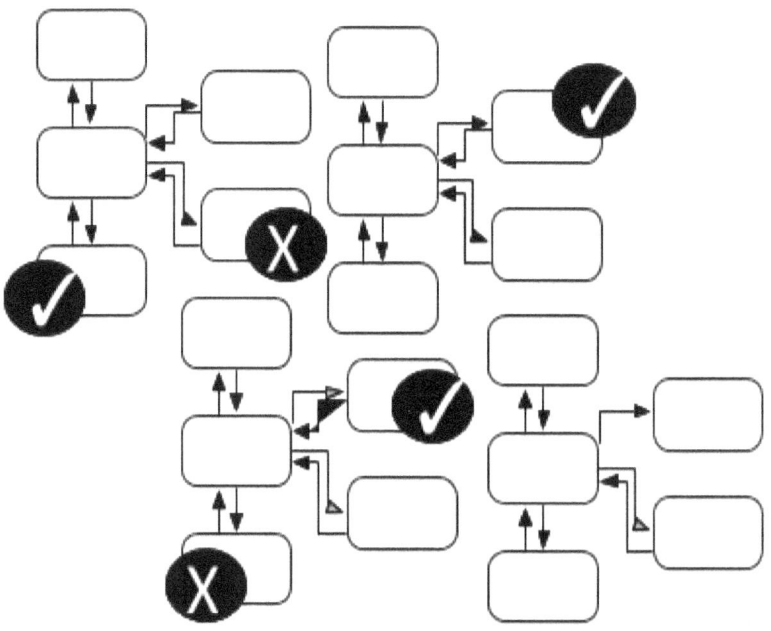

- Many CI tools
- Team Foundation Server
- TeamCity
- Many more!

- Desired features

- Cross platform
  - Windows builders, Java builders and others

- Source control integration
- Notifications
- IDE Integration (optional)

- Map a microservice to a CI build
  - Code change triggers build of specific service
  - Feedback just received on that service
  - Builds and tests run quicker
  - Separate code repository for service
  - End product is in one place
  - CI builds to test database changes
  - Both microservice build and database upgrade are ready

- Avoid one CI build for all services

In this section of the module, we're going to look at the automation tools that are available for our microservices architecture in the form of Continuous Integration tools and Continuous Deployment tools. We've seen the previous module why we need Continuous Integration tools for our microservices architecture. The good news is, there are many Continuous Integration tools, from Team Foundation Server to TeamCity, and many more. You just need to Google for Continuous Integration tools and you'll see how many there are. When making your selection, these are some of the desired features that you should look for. The tools should be cross platform, so if you build microservices using Windows technologies or Java technologies, it has the relevant builders in order to produce a build. You also need to ensure that it integrates with your chosen source control system so that when you check a code change in, it can detect this and trigger off a build. It also must have the functionality to send notifications. So, for example, if your integration tests fail, it must have the ability to alert and send notifications. It's also nice to have a Continuous Integration tool that has some integration with the Development ID. Another key thing is, when you use Continuous Integration tools, you map microservices to individual CI builds. In this way, a code change for a specific microservice only triggers the build for that specific service, and this way if the build fails, you know the feedback is just received for a specific service, and you know where the issue lies. The feedback is also received quite quickly because it's just one microservice that is built, the test and the build run a lot faster. As well as having a separate CI build for a microservice, it's also worth having a separate code repository for a service. This way, two microservices are not accidentally changed at the same time. Another advantage of mapping a microservice to a CI build is we can place the microservice in a specific place, which helps with continuous deployment. Because a microservices will also have its own database and a microservice maps to a specific CI build, we can configure the CI build to also test the database changes, and this way the CI build can also ready both the microservice build and the database upgrade at the same time. If you choose to have one CI build for all your microservices, you will lose all these advantages we've just described, so you should avoid having one CI build for all your services. Instead, each microservice should have its own CI build. And remember, microservices should be independently changeable and deployable, and having a specific CI build for each microservice helps this.

## Automation Tools: Continuous Deployment

- Many CD tools
- Aim for cross platform tools

- Desired features
- Central control panel

- **Simple to add deployment targets**
- **Support for scripting**
- **Support for build statuses**
- **Integration with CI tool**
- **Support for multiple environments**
- **Support for PAAS**

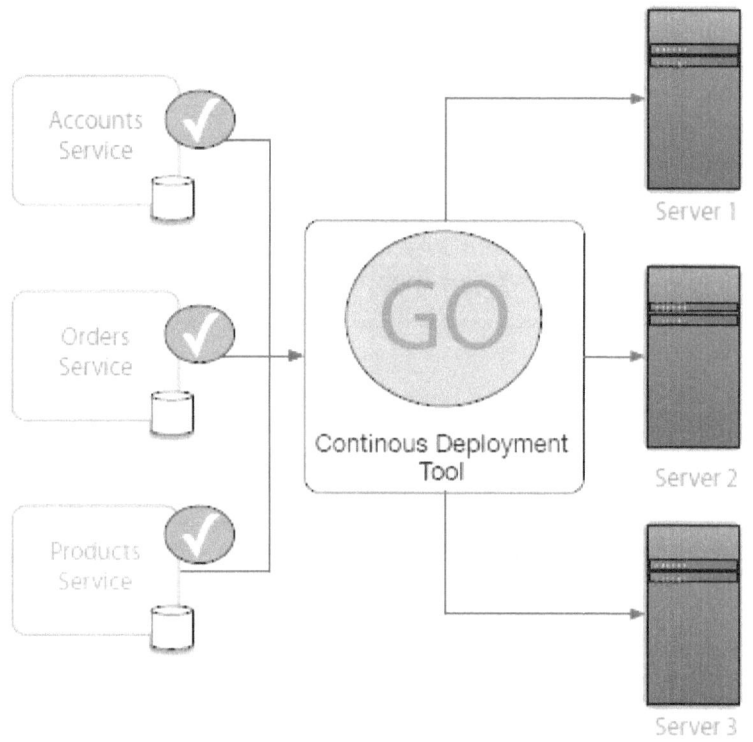

**And like there are many Continuous Integration tools, there are also many**

Continuous Deployment tools, and like with the Continuous Integration tools, we need to ensure that our Continuous Deployment tool is cross platform so that it can help us deploy our microservices to a Windows server, or for example, a Linux server. Other desired features for Continuous Deployment tools are the option to have a central control panel. Having a distributed architecture like a microservices architecture can make the deployment of software quite complex. Having a central control panel just makes things a little bit easier. We need a clear way of seeing what production environments we have and what test environments we have that we can deploy our software to, and it must be a straightforward task to add extra deployment targets. So these are deployment targets where our software is delivered, so these might be virtual machines containers or actual physical machines. And the task of deployment is always not straightforward, it's not always as simple as just copying files across, and therefore, sometimes we need scripting to do additional ad-hoc tasks. It's also useful if our Continuous Deployment tool has support for build statuses. So if a build fails during continuous integration due to failing tests, it knows how to highlight this and how not to include it in a production release list, and therefore, it's ideal if our Continuous Deployment tool has some kind of integration with our Continuous Integration tool, so not only to see build statuses, but also to know where to fetch the build from. We must also ensure that our Continuous Deployment tool can support multiple environments, so for example, a production environment and a test environment, but we must also ensure that our Continuous Deployment tool can release to cloud-based hosted system, for example, Microsoft Azure and Amazon Web Services. And when it comes to microservices architecture, it's key that our Continuous Deployment tool is as flexible as it can be because with microservices we could end up using any type of technology platform.

## Module Summary

- Communication
  - Synchronous
  - Asynchronous
- Platforms
  - Hosting
  - Virtualization
  - Containers
  - Self Hosting
  - Registry and Discovery

**Microservices**
- Observable
- Monitoring Tech
- Logging Tech

- Performance
- Scaling
- Caching
- API Gateway

**Tools**
- Automation
- Continuous Integration
- Continuous Deployment

In this module, we've looked at the communication technologies that can be used with microservices. We looked at synchronous communication technologies and we also looked at asynchronous communication technologies, and we concluded that in your microservices architecture you'll probably end up using a combination of both. We also looked at technologies that we could use to host our microservices, from virtual machines, to containers, to self-hosting. And we also looked at how we could have our microservices register themselves and be discovered. We concluded with the fact that in a microservices architecture you're bound to create multiple instances of a microservice as the demand increases, and therefore, you need a way of registering these instances so that they can be discovered, and that in a self-hosted systems registry and discovery is your responsibility. We also looked at the desired features for monitoring technology and logging technology that would make our microservices more observable. We also looked at the scaling and caching and API Gateway technology that's available to help with microservices performance. We also looked at the desired features for our automation tools that make our microservices architecture easier to test and deploy. In the next module, we will look at how we can move forward with a microservices architecture when in a brownfield situation and when in a greenfield situation.

# Module 4 : Moving forward with microservices

Overview

- Module
- Brownfield Microservices

- Greenfield Microservices
- Microservices Provisos

# Introduction

In this module we will look at how you can move forwards with a microservices architecture when you're in a brownfield situation, meaning that there's an existing system with an existing architecture that needs to be migrated to a microservices architecture. We will also look at how you can move forwards with a microservices architecture in a greenfield situation, in a situation where you're creating a system from scratch. We will then conclude the module by looking at microservices provisos, basically, everything you need to understand and accept before you can move forwards with a microservices architecture.

# Brownfield Microservices: Approach | Migration | Database Migration | Transactions | Reporting

## Brownfield Microservices: Approach

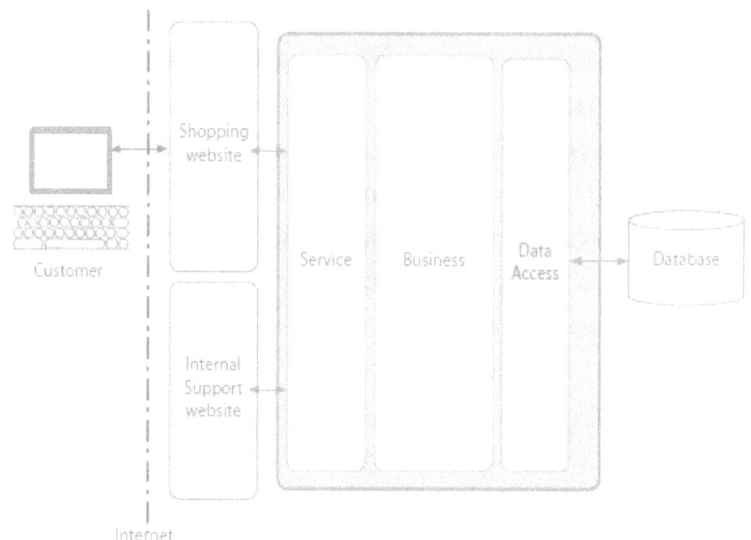

- 
- Existing system
- Monolithic system
- Organically grown
- Seems to large to split

- Lacks microservices design principles
  - Identify seams
  - Separation that reflects domains
  - Identify bounded contexts
- Start modularising the bounded contexts
  - Move code incrementally
  - Tidy up a section per release
    - Take your time
    - Existing functionality needs to remain intact
  - Run unit tests and integration tests to validate change
  - Keep reviewing
- Seams are future microservice boundaries

We'll start off by looking at how we can move forwards with a microservices architecture in a brownfield situation. We will first look at the initial approach we can take in order to ready our system for the migration over to a microservices architecture. We will then look at the actual migration of how we can migrate a monolithic system to a microservices architectured system. A monolithic system is also likely to have one large database so we will also look at database migration, database migration from a monolithic database to a number of databases to support our microservices. We will then go on to look at the affect microservices architecture can have on transactions within our system and reporting within our system. So in a brownfield situation, our existing system is likely to be a monolithic systems that's organically grown, and it might seem too large to split into microservices. It's also likely to have one large business layer or domain layer where most of the business logic for the system exists, and overall the system probably lacks most of the microservices design principles we've covered in this course. So the question is, how can we start readying this system for migration from a monolithic system to a microservices architectured system? The first key step is to start analyzing the code within the system.

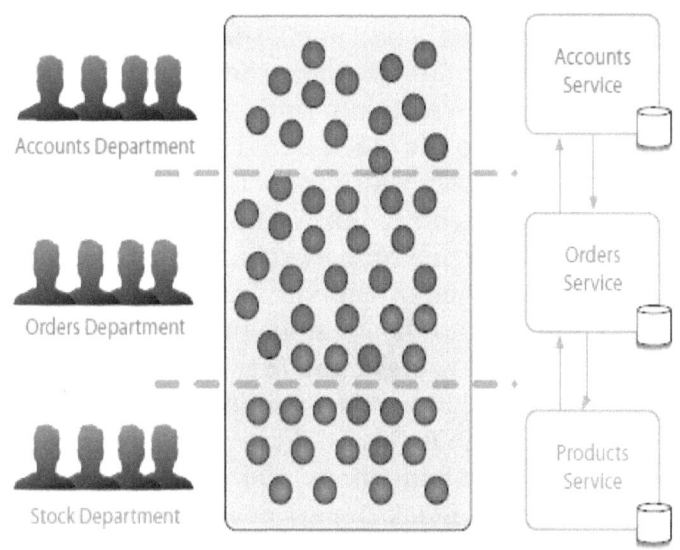

We'll then start identifying seams within the system, and this is done by identifying separation within the code which reflects the domains within our business. And within the code, it might be clear to see specific classes, modules, and functions which relate to specific parts of the organization, and the separation might not be just related to domains within the organization, but functions within the actual organization. So, for example, you might see _____ loads of code related to the Accounts Department within your system, but you might also see _____ loads of code related to a specific function within the business, for example, calculating postage costs. And the seams of both scenarios are valid, and by grouping our code in business domains and business functions, we're basically identifying bounded contexts within our system, an idea which is taken from domain-driven design about grouping related code together. You also might find that seams within the system are not that clear at all, they're quite fuzzy because of overlapping code. So, for example, you might find code which is related to the Stock Department overlaps significantly with code related to the Orders Department, so this is where we need to start readying our code by refactoring the code so that it's better split into bonded contexts. We can start off by creating a module for each bounded context, and then we can start moving our code around incrementally. So, for example, this might involve moving classes and functions, which actually should be in the Stock Department related code, away from the Orders Department code, and moving into a module which represents the Stock Department. So, for example, in a .NET project we might have an Accounts project, an Orders project, a Stock project, each creating code libraries which are part of our overall solution. We then move the overlapping code by moving the overlapping functions and classes which are in the wrong place to the right module or library. Remember, you can tidy up each section per release. You need to take your time, because we need to ensure that we don't break the existing system. And to validate your code refactoring, it's important to run unit tests and integration tests to validate your change, and if you're not using unit tests or integration tests, it might be worth investing in unit test and integration test technology. The other key thing is after every release we review the code again, and refactor again, and make our bounded contexts even more clear. It's important to have clear seams and clear bounded contexts, because in the future these are our microservice boundaries, and in the next section of the module we will start looking at how we can migrate these bounded contexts into actual microservices.

# Brownfield Microservices: Migration

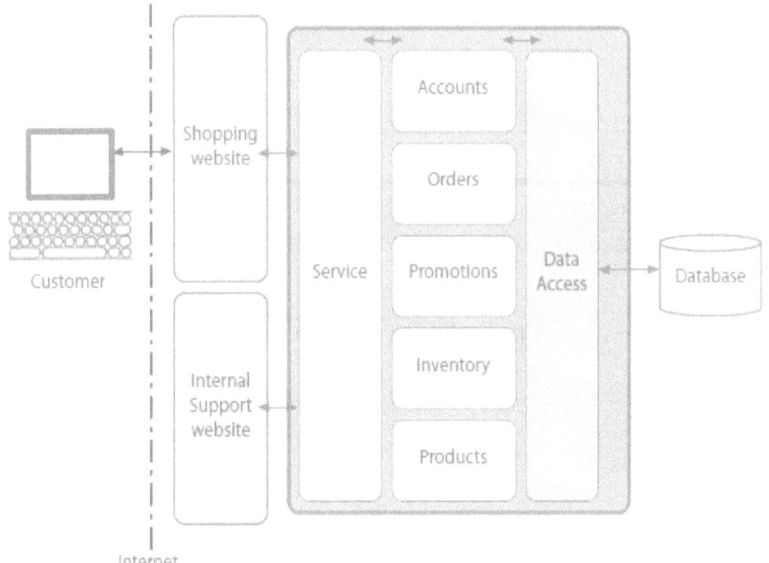

- Code is organised into bounded contexts
  - Code related to a business domain or function is in one place
  - Clear boundaries with clear interfaces between each

- Convert bounded contexts into microservices
  - Start off with one
    - Use to get comfortable
  - Make it switchable
    - Maintain two versions of the code
  - How to prioritise what to split?
    - By risk
    - By technology
    - By dependencies
  - Incremental approach
  - Integrating with the monolithic
    - Monitor both for impact
    - Monitor operations that talk to microservices
    - Review and improve infrastructure

- Incrementally the monolithic will be converted

In the previous section of the module, you saw how we ready our code, how we reorganize our code so that it's ready for migration over into microservices. In this section of the module, you will see the steps we can take in order to migrate that code into actual microservices. So when our code has been reorganized into bounded contexts, code related to a specific business domain or function is in one place, and there are clear boundaries with clear interfaces between each. So, for example, if there's a function within the Orders section of the code that needs the Account section of the code to do something, there are clear functions and methods defined that the Order section needs to call in order for the Account section of the code to do something. There are clear interfaces between the two bounded contexts, and it's these bounded contexts that we convert into a microservice.

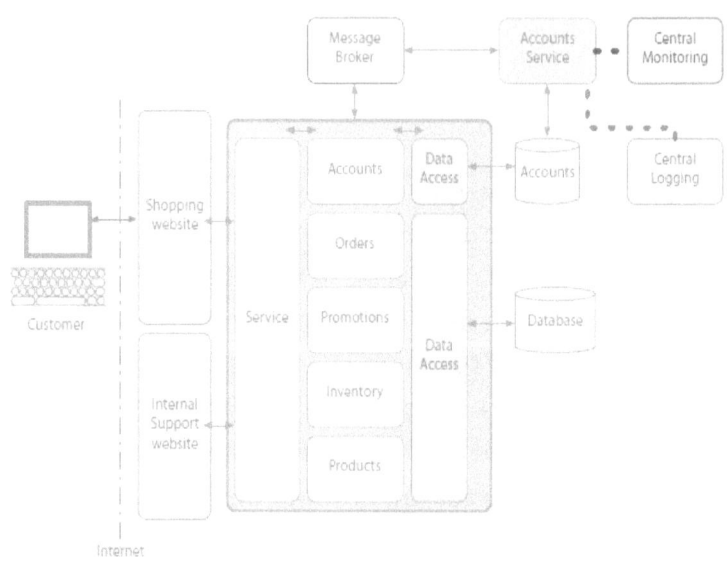

We might initially start off by just converting one into a microservice. This is so that we can get comfortable with the microservices architecture and the technology that it involves, for example, message brokers, central monitoring tools, central logging tools, continuous integration and deployment tools, as well as getting comfortable with other things like distributed transactions, which actually complete over the network, and things like separate data stores for specific parts of the system. You could even make the old functionality and the new microservices functionality switchable, so if there are any issues you can revert back to the old functionality, however, the risk with this is you might end up maintaining two variations of the same code. So how do you prioritize what to split at first into a microservice? You might do this be risk. So the part of the system which has least impact if there's an issue, you might choose to split that out into a microservice first, or you might do this by technology. If there's a specific part of the system that, for example, could do with a different type of technology in order to improve performance or provide extra features, you might choose to split that part of the system out first or you might do this by dependencies, converting the bounded context with the least amount of dependencies into a microservice first. So, for example, if the Promotions bounded context is only ever called by the Orders bounded context, it might be safer to convert the Promotions bounded context into a microservice first. The key thing to remember is we want to take an incremental approach so that we can learn how to live with the microservices architecture. And because it's an incremental approach, we need to ensure the new microservices we create they integrate with our existing monolithic system, and when the two types of architecture run alongside each other, we need to monitor both for impact. For example, how is the monolithic system coping with having some of the transactions done over the network. You might choose to closely monitor operations that specifically talk to microservices, and you might review each time and improve the infrastructure in order to support the new distributed transactions which are done by the microservices. And by taking this incremental approach to converting the monolithic, eventually it will be converted to a complete microservices architectured system. In the next section of the module, we will look at how we can split our monolithic database into databases for each microservice.

# Brownfield Microservices: Database Migration

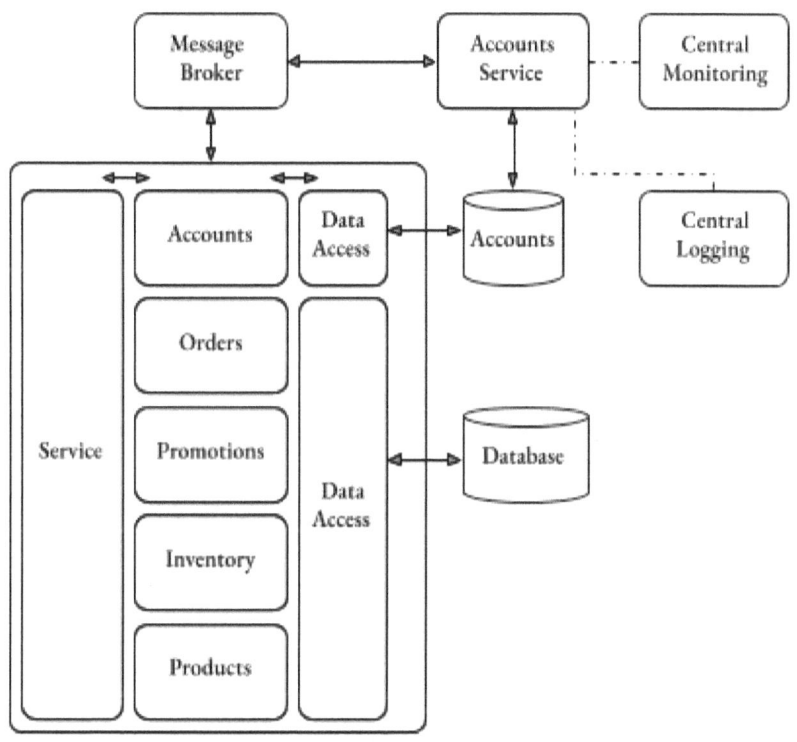

- Avoid shared databases
- Split databases using seams
- Relate tables to code seams
- Supporting the existing application
- Data layer that connects to

- multiple database
- Tables that link across seams
- API calls that can fetch that data for a relationship
- Refactor database into multiple databases
- Data referential integrity
- Static data tables
- Shared data

In this section of the module, we will look at how we can split our monolithic database across our microservices so that each microservice has its own database. In a previous module, we've already mentioned the fact that we want to avoid shared databases. We want our microservices to be independently changeable and independently deployable, and a shared database does not allow this. So the question is, how do we split our databases? The good news is it's the same approach as we took to split the code into bounded contexts. We basically identify seams in the databases, seams which relate to seams in the code. So, for example, we might have tables which relate to the Accounts Department functionality, and therefore, that is a clear seam and we can split those tables out into a separate database. And in order to support the existing application, the monolithic application, you might have a data layer which can access multiple databases. So what do we do when we have a table which links across seams? For example, you might have a Promotion which links to an Order. This is where the service, so for example, our Promotion Service, must provide methods which allow the Order Service to fetch a specific Promotions data from the Promotion Service. This kind of approach will allow our microservices to fetch any data that's related to one of its entities from any other microservices, and like we refactored our code base into multiple code bases, we are basically doing the same within a database. We're refactoring the database into multiple databases. Even though we've refactored our database into multiple databases, we still have to worry about data referential integrity. So, for example, in our Accounts microservice, if I delete the account of a customer, I also might want to delete related orders for that customer, orders that exist in the Orders microservice, and I would do this by calling the Orders microservice and calling a method which basically instructs the Orders microservice to delete specific orders related to a specific account ID. So data referential integrity can be maintained even though the data is split across microservices, by having the microservices talk to each other and instruct each other. So what if you have static data tables that are required by all microservices? The best thing to do with this kind of static data is to place that static data within a configuration file and make that configuration file available to each microservice. The other option for static data tables is to have a specific microservice just for them, so other microservices can just basically call that service in order to fetch that static data. The same is valid for shared data, data that's read and written by multiple microservices. Promote this data to its own microservice, so that the other microservices can interact with it in order to read and write that data. In the next section of the module, we will look at how we need to think differently about transactions when migrating from a monolithic system to a microservices architectured system.

# Brownfield Microservices: Transactions

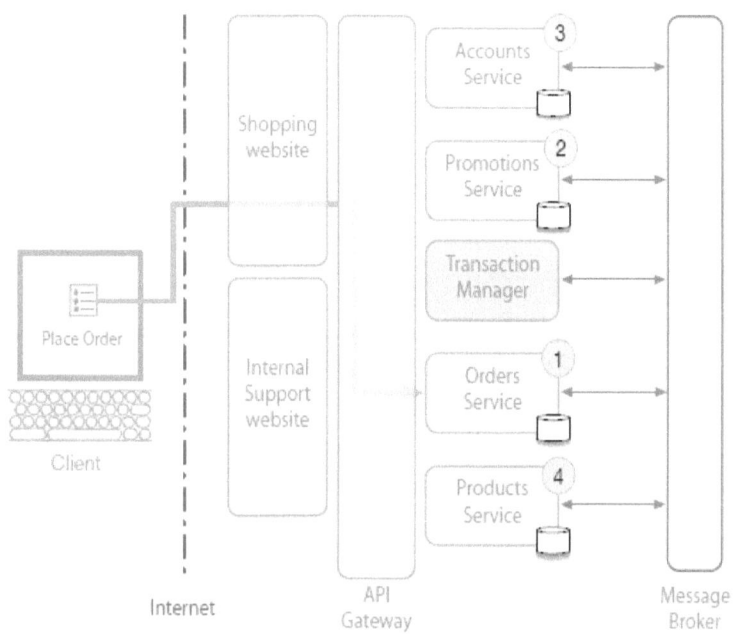

- **Transactions ensure data integrity**
- **Transactions are simple in monolithic applications**
- **Transactions spanning microservices are complex**
  - **Complex to observe**
  - **Complex to problem solve**
  - **Complex to rollback**
  - **Options for failed transactions**

- Try again later
- Abort entire transaction
- Use a transaction manager
  - Two phase commit
- Disadvantage of transaction manager
  - Reliance on transaction manager
  - Delay in processing
  - Potential bottleneck
  - Complex to implement
- Distributed transaction compatibility
  - Completed message for the monolith

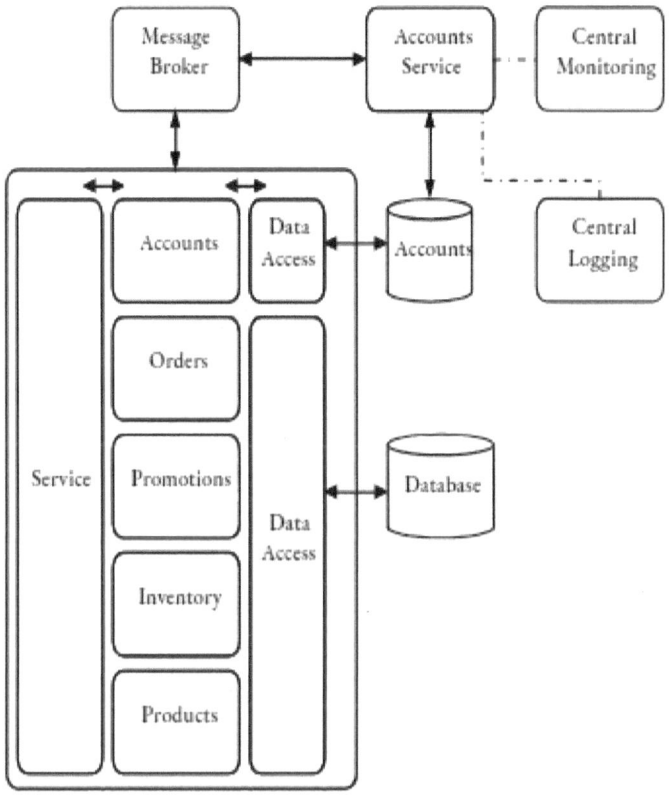

In this section of the module, we'll look at how we need to view and handle transactions within our system differently when moving from a monolithic system to a microservices architectured system. Firstly, transactions are useful. They ensure data integrity. They basically allow us to create or update several records as part of one transaction, and if one of those updates or creates fails, we can roll the entire transaction back, and our monolithic system transactions are fairly straightforward. You have one process which is updating and creating the records which are part of the transaction, and therefore, the same process can either commit the transaction or roll the transaction back if there are any issues. However, in a microservices system, transactions are complex because you now have several processes, i.e., several microservices which actually complete the one transaction. The transaction is now a distributed transaction which spans multiple microservices, and therefore it's complex to observe and to problem solve, and complex to roll back. In our example here, we have a transaction of placing an order, and as you can see, it starts off within the Orders microservice and then we create or update a record using the Promotions microservice, and then we create an update or record using the Account microservice, and then the transaction finishes off by creating or updating a record within the Products microservice. So if one of these microservices fails to update or create a record which is part of our distributed transaction, we will need to rollback the entire transaction. So what are the options for failed transactions? One option is we can try again later. So the part of the transaction which has failed, we place back onto the queue for possibly another service to pick up. The transaction will then eventually complete. This, however, relies on the other instance of the microservice not failing the same part of the transaction. Another option is we abort the entire transaction. We detect the fact that our transaction has failed, and then we issue an Undo transaction. And Undo transaction basically tells all of the microservices to undo any creates or updates which they carried out as part of a specific transaction. The problem with this is, who issues the undo transaction, and what if the Undo transaction itself fails? One way of resolving our transaction issues is to use transaction manager software. Some transaction manager software use a method called two phase commit, and in this method all participating microservices first tell the transaction manager if they are okay to commit to their part of the transaction, and if they all are, the transaction manager tells all participating microservices to commit the transaction, and if any of the microservices participating in the distributed transaction does not respond or responds with a no to committing, then the transaction manager tells all participating microservices to rollback the transaction. The problem with the use of a transaction manager is that we become heavily reliant on the transaction manager, and it also delays the processing of our transactions, and it potentially also might become a bottleneck within the system. The transaction manager can also be quite complex to implement. Another thing we need to worry about is, the fact that when we run our new microservices alongside our monolithic system, our new microservice needs to tell the monolithic system that their part of the transaction is complete, and this can be achieved by placing a message in the message queue for the monolithic system. In the next section of the module, we will look at the effects of migrating to a microservices architecture on reporting within our system.

## Brownfield Microservices: Reporting

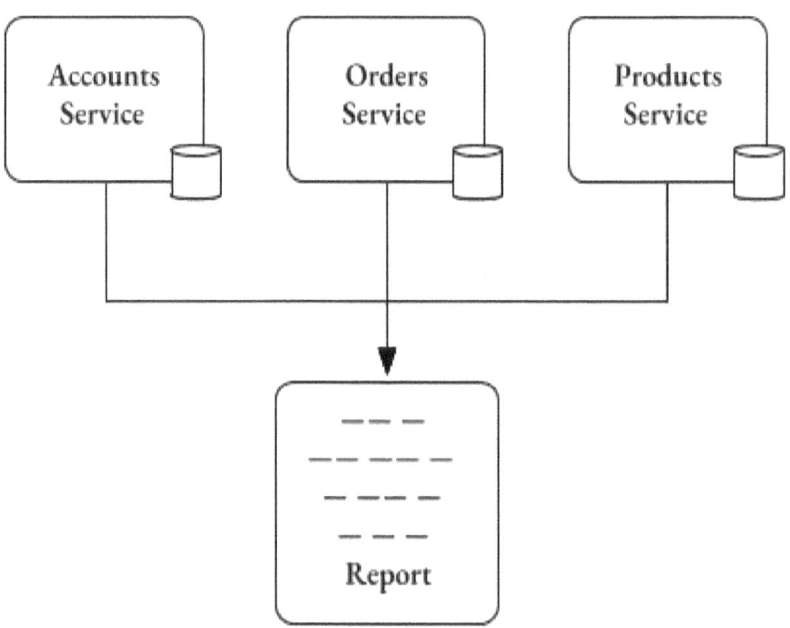

- Microservices complicate reporting
  - Data split across microservices
  - No central database
  - Joining data across databases
  - Slower reporting
  - Complicate report development

- Possible solutions
  - Service calls for report data
  - Data dumps
  - Consolidation environment

In this section of the module, we're going to look at how we can support reporting within our system when we have a microservices architectured system. Microservices do complicate reporting. In a monolithic system you might have a few databases that you need to report from, but in a microservices architectured system, each microservice has its own database. The data you want to report on is basically split across multiple microservices, and by default there is no central database that you can extract the reporting data from, and there will be inevitable need to join data across databases in order to provide the information your organization needs, and we will have to accept the fact that reporting within a microservices architectured system will be slower, and it will be complicated to develop an actual report.

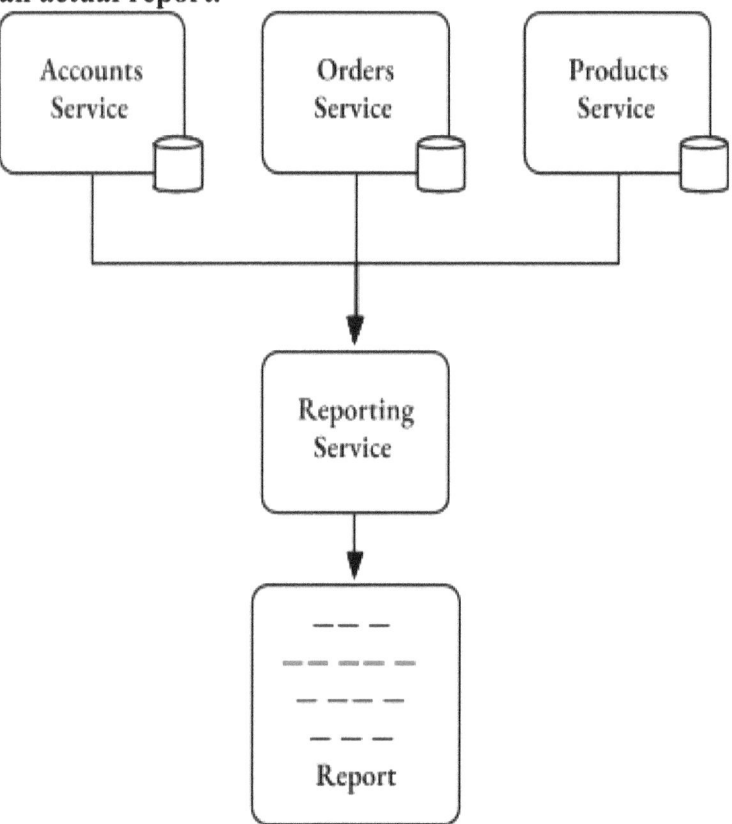

However, there are some solutions which make things easier. We could, for example, have a dedicated reporting service which basically calls other microservices to collect the data and to consolidate the data, so that it can be presented in a report. However, this might not be adequate if we're reporting on large volumes of data or if we need our reporting to be real-time.

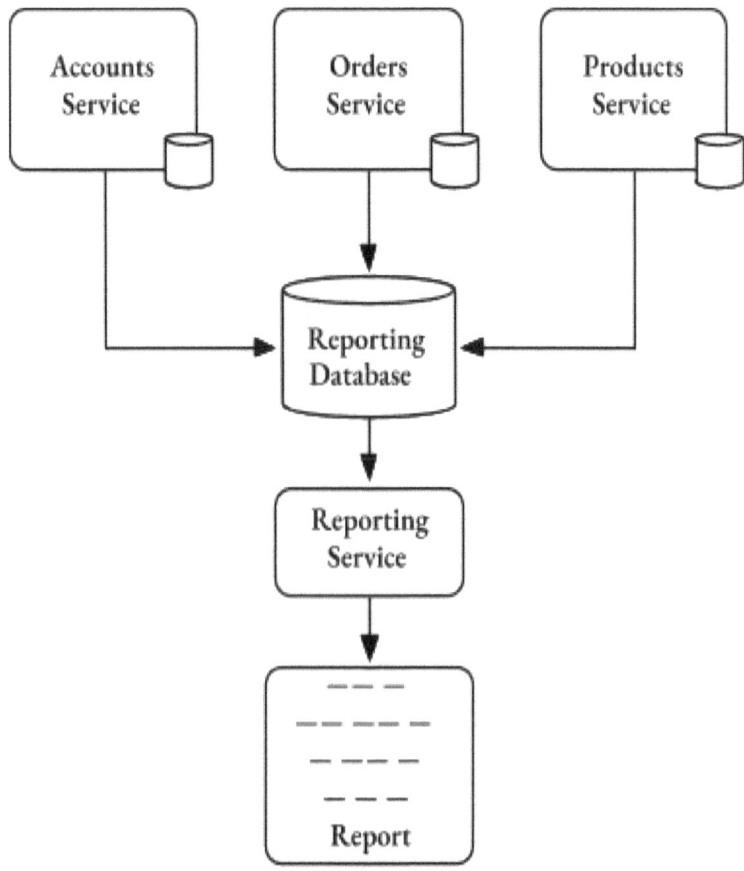

Another option is that we have a data dump, a data dump which basically dumps the data to a central database that can be used for reporting purposes. How you implement the data dump will depend on your requirements. For example, do you need the data in real-time? If real-time data is not a requirement, what you could do is you could have a consolidation environment where all the data from all the microservices is consolidated into a central database. This can be done, for example, using an _____ job. So in order for our microservices architecture to be successful, we need to ensure we have some kind of reporting strategy.

## Greenfield Microservices : Introduction | Approach

## Greenfield Microservices: Introduction

- New project
- Evolving requirements
- Business domain
- Not fully understood
- Getting domain experts involved
- System boundaries will evolve
- Teams experience

| | | |
|---|---|---|
| | • | First microservice |
| | • | Experienced with microservices |
| integration | • | Existing system |
| | • | Monolithic system |
| | • | Established microservices architecture |
| change | • | Push for |
| | • | Changes to apply microservice principles |

# Greenfield Microservices: Approach

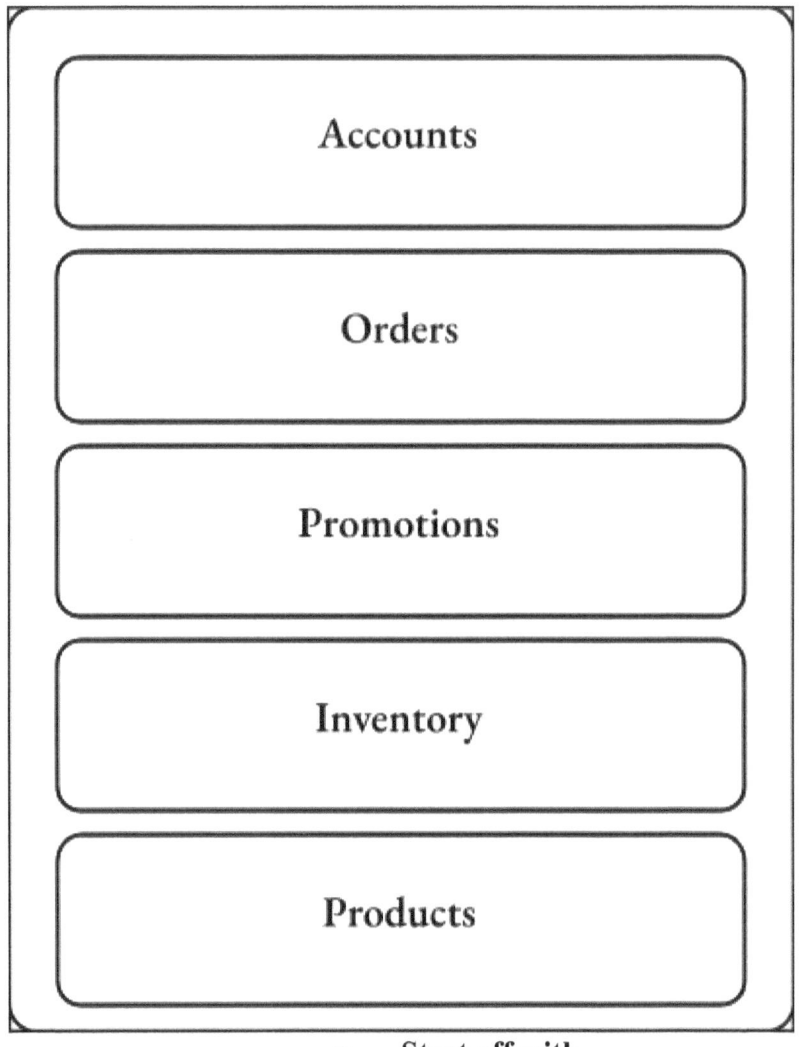

- Start off with monolithic design
- High level
- Evolving seams

- Develop areas into modules
- Boundaries start to become clearer
- Refine and refactor design
- Split further when required
- Modules become services
- Shareable code libraries promote to service
- Review microservice principles at each stage
- Prioritise by
- Minimal viable product
- Customer needs and demand

In this section of the module, we will look at how we can approach our microservices architecture in a greenfield situation, where basically we're creating a new system from scratch. So a greenfield situation will most likely involve a new project. It might be a new aspect of our existing system, or it might be a completely new system altogether, and as with all new systems, the requirements might evolve during the design phase, and there might be no clear indicator indicating what microservice is actually required for the overall solution. And this will mainly happen because this is a new system, and the business domain is not fully understand, and we have to get the domain experts involved in order to understand it. We will also find, as we discuss and design with the domain experts, the system boundaries will evolve. The initial boundaries you set will change, and that's why it's important in a greenfield situation to understand and collect the requirements, and not focus too much on what microservices are required to address the overall problem. How well the design and discussions go will also depend on the team's experience. Is this the team's first microservices architectured system, or have they got experience with microservices? The other key thing to understand is, is the new system going to integrate with an existing system, and is the current system a monolithic system, or do you already have an established microservices architectured system. The key thing to remember is we need to push for change. We need to change in order to apply our microservices principles if there's currently no microservices architectured system. The irony, however, is that because the requirements are evolving, and it's not quite clear to see what microservices are required, it's best to start off with a monolithic design, so we start off with a high level design, and we allow the seams within our system to evolve. We define each high level area as a module, and as the interaction between these areas and seams becomes clearer, the boundaries within our system start to become clearer as well. And as our understanding of these modules, these areas, becomes clearer, we refine and refactor our design, and if we need to further split a module we split it further. Eventually these modules should represent business domains and business functions on a very finite granular level. And it's these modules that later on go on to become our microservices. If you find there's loads of code that needs to be shared between these modules, consider promoting those code libraries to a service. The key thing to remember is that each stage we review our microservice principles, and that we also keep the requirements in mind, we actually deliver what's required in terms of customer needs and demand.

# Microservices Provisos

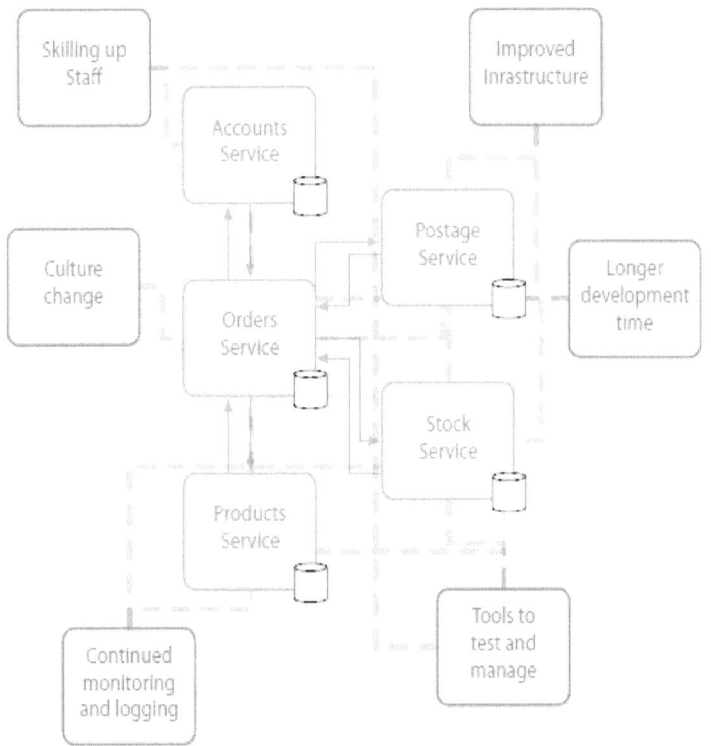

- Accepting initial expense
- Longer development times
- Cost and training for tools and new skills
- Skilling up for distributed systems

- Handling distributed transactions
- Handling reporting
- Additional testing resource
- Latency and performance testing
- Testing for resilience
- Improving infrastructure
- Security
- Performance
- Reliance
- Overhead to manage microservices
- Cloud technologies
- Culture change

In this section of the module, we'll look at microservices provisos, basically what you need to accept before you implement a microservices architecture. If it's your first microservices system, you need to accept the fact that there will be some initial expense. The development times will be longer, and there will be a need for training for tools and new skills to cope with a new microservices architectured system. We also need to accept the fact that it will take our team time to scale up to handle a distributed system. Only with experience will they learn how to handle distributed transactions and how to problem solve distributed transactions, as well as handling reporting in an environment where the data is not kept in one place. And because of the distributed nature of the system, you might also need to invest in extra testing resource in order to test for latency, performance, and resilience. This is important, because remember, our software is no longer a single process, instead it's a number of components which are distributed over a system, and they work together over the network, and therefore it's important to have extra \_\_\_\_\_ who have the skills to test for network network-related issues, as well as investing in testing the network infrastructure. You might find you have to improve the network infrastructure in terms of security, performance, and reliance. And, again, this is important because our software heavily relies on the network in order to function. The components need to interact with each other in a timely manner in order for our software to function, therefore, we need to ensure that our infrastructure is adequate for the complex distributed piece of software, which is what our microservices architecture is. We need to ensure that we understand that there will be an overhead to manage these microservices. We need to constantly monitor our system for performance issues to avoid any problems. We also need to accept the fact that investing in cloud technologies will make the management of microservices a lot easier. We also need to accept the fact that applying the microservices design principles, overall for an organization, is a culture change.

## Module Summary

- Brownfield Microservices
- Greenfield Microservices
- Microservices Provisos

In this module, we looked at how we can architect a microservices system when in a brownfield situation, i.e., where there's an existing system that needs to be converted. We looked at how we need to reorganize our existing code base into bounded contexts, which are then later on converted into microservices. We also looked at how we can create a microservices system in a greenfield situation, where basically we're creating a new system from scratch. We concluded with the fact that it's best to start off with a monolithic design which you refine and refactor into a microservices design. We concluded the module by looking at microservices provisos, basically everything we need to accept before we introduce a microservices architectured system. We concluded with the fact that not only is microservices a technical change for a company, but it's also a huge culture change for a company.

www.ingramcontent.com/pod-product-compliance
Lightning Source LLC
Chambersburg PA
CBHW031623210526
45464CB00004B/1721